VISUAL chronicles

THE NO-FEAR GUIDE TO CREATING ART JOURNALS, CREATIVE MANIFESTOS & ALTERED BOOKS

LINDA WOODS +
KAREN DININO

NORTH LIGHT BOOKS
Cincinnati, Ohio

www.artistsnetwork.com

10 09 08 07 06   5 4 3 2 1

Distributed in Canada by Fraser Direct
100 Armstrong Avenue
Georgetown, ON, Canada L7G 5S4

Distributed in the U.K. and Europe by David & Charles
Brunel House, Newton Abbot, Devon, TQ12 4PU, England
Tel: (+44) 1626 323200, Fax: (+44) 1626 323319
E-mail: mail@davidandcharles.co.uk

Distributed in Australia by Capricorn Link
P.O. Box 704, Windsor, NSW 2756 Australia

fw
F+W PUBLICATIONS, INC.

Editor: Tonia Davenport
Cover Designer: Karla Baker
Designer & Layout Artist: Marissa Bowers
Production Coordinator: Robin Richie
Photographers: Christine Polomsky, Al Parrish,
                        Tim Grondin and Hal Barkan
Photo Stylist: Jan Nickum

Library of Congress Cataloging-in-Publication Data

Woods, Linda

Visual chronicles : the no-fear guide to creating art journals,
creative manifestos, and altered books / Linda Woods and Karen Dinino.

     p. cm.

Includes index.

ISBN 1-58180-770-8 (pbk. : alk. paper)

1. Handicraft. 2. Scrapbook journaling. I. Dinino, Karen. II. Title.

TT157.W637 2006

702'.8'1--dc22

                              2005019278

About the Authors

Linda Woods's vibrant artwork, unique journals, and articles about the creative process have been featured in books, magazines, art calendars and exhibits worldwide. Karen Dinino practices law, trains executives to write and speak well, and formerly was a professional journalist. Together, Linda and Karen teach workshops designed to help artists communicate better with words and to help writers communicate better with art—the combination creating powerful, evocative, limitless visual journals.

When they aren't traveling the globe, adding new candy wrappers to their journals, Karen and Linda live in Southern California. To the delight of their husbands, they no longer live together. Linda lives with her husband, Dustin, and Karen lives with her husband, Bill, and their two children, Emily and Brent. Linda and Karen can usually be found instant messaging each other in the wee hours of the night.

To learn more, visit their Web sites at:
www.sistersonsojourn.com and www.visualchronicles.com

To see more of Linda's inspirational artwork,
visit: www.colormetrue.com

For great advice on crossing the legal minefield facing employers (or for great writing tips, in general) visit Karen at: www.employmentor.net

Dedication

For Dustin, my apple tree, my brightness.
And for Karen, who shares my dreams and always leaves me the last bite.

Linda

For Bill, Emily, Brent and Grayson, who have left my Wish Box empty.
And for Linda, who gave me the heart to keep wishing.

Karen

Acknowledgments

An abundance of gratitude to Sujata, for giving Linda her first set of pens . . . and to Anea, for helping her break her attachment to them! To our families and friends, who appear in our journals: Thank you for inspiring us on paper and in life.

Many thanks to Tricia Waddell for believing in the creative power of two sisters, and to Tonia Davenport for guiding us on our journey, with laughter and chocolate to spare. We truly appreciate Christine Polomsky, Al Parrish, Marissa Bowers and Karla Baker, who captured our essence in color and mixed media. And a thank you to Jennie Dunham and Matt Thompson for their kind counsel and encouragement early on!

Sisters

happy ones.

contents

This area seems so colorless and bland. No gothic churches, no fjords, no lush gardens, no waterfalls or babbling rivers running through town. My daydreams will be of those things. I will bathe the house in rich colors to remind me of my journey. Walking into remind me of my journey. Walking into the kitchen will be like walking in the Piazza San Marco. The hall bathroom will be Florence! And, our bedroom Chelsea Blue. Singapore for the living room and Norway in the loft.

NOT GOOD at CATCHING things

a good journey

GET

A HOLE IN THE DISH gLove

MORE SLEEP

AFRAID OF THE DEEP END

i

We are stranded.

my uniform

black shorts that look like a

SOMETIMES WE EAT BREAKFAST FOR DINNER

EXPLORE

EVERY DAY IS AN ARTFUL JOURNEY

It's time for you to let all your personalities come out to play. Yes, *YOU*. Spontaneous, unedited, fresh and in bold color. Who you've been, who you are, who you pretend to be and who you dare to become. Join us on an artful sojourn into your head, your heart and your dreams to discover the many, many ways that *YOU* are *ART!* *Visual Chronicles* is about transferring your essence to the surface, whatever that surface may be, and whatever part of your vast essence you draw on at any creative moment. Anyone can make an artistic visual journal, and it can be in any form you want. Yes, we meant both those things: *any* one, *any* form. (See, it's already getting easier!)

The real news of our lives is not in newspapers. *We* must chronicle our own adventures and achievements, our brilliant observations and our comic relief, our best friends and our greatest embarrassments. Your journal doesn't have to be cute or happy or provocative (but just try to make it boring; it's impossible), and you don't need to travel to glamorous locations for material to write about, sketch or collage. Every day, you embark on a journey. It could be a journey to exotic foreign lands, or, more likely, a journey to the grocery store at midnight for milk.

You can capture your journey even if you think you lack artistic or writing skills and have no free time. Just "bust" any fears blocking your creative expression and collect the fallout as art. We'll do it with you—so-called mistakes and all! Whether you are initially comfortable with art or with words, it is laugh-out-loud fun to combine these expressive forms to create art journals, creative manifestos and altered books that record or share *YOU*. Let's get going!

0009336869001

Start today. You can journal with supplies you already have on hand. *YOU* will *POP* off the page whether you create with cheap ink pens or fine oil pastels. It's fun to build a collection of inks, stamps, paints and decorative papers, but you can express volumes with scissors, tape and newspaper, too. Introspection is your primary tool for journaling, and digging through your kitchen, laundry room and desk drawers will probably yield many other supplies you need.

What to use?

PAINTS AND INKS

Inexpensive acrylic craft paints in 2-ounce (59ml) bottles are our favorites. We often blend these paints with glazing medium. For watercolors, we use small tubes or Peerless watercolor paint cards. We tend to use dye-based inkpads for stamping and sponging, and we particularly like the inkpads by Memories. For travel and inking the edges of tags, Petal Points and Paintbox pads by ColorBox are great. We basecoat pages with gesso, when needed.

PENS AND PENCILS

Sharpie fine-point permanent ink pens work great for writing, and they come in a rainbow of colors. For drawing, Marvy Marker Dual Tip pens, in permanent ink, are versatile and portable. We aren't picky about pencils.

BRUSHES AND APPLICATORS

Flat brushes in 1", ⅜" and ½" (3cm, 10mm and 12mm) sizes give good surface coat options. Scruffy brushes are great for texture—a #4 is good. Try using cosmetic sponges; they work miracles with either inkpads or paint.

RUBBER STAMPS

Alphabet stamps in a variety of sizes make journaling easier. An assortment of rubber stamp images inspires you and "draws" for you.

STENCILS

The easiest way to add texture is with stencils. You can get stencil packs for collaging at craft stores, and you can even use household items, like notebook paper holes for dots, or mesh drywall tape for grids. You can also use hole punches to make your own stencils.

PAPER PUNCHES

Geometric-shaped paper punches can create a variety of patterns in your journals. It's easy to cut out multiple shapes with a punch, or to punch some images to bring with you to journal on the go.

ADHESIVES

We like Uhu Stic glue sticks the best for dry glue. When gluing dimensional items, gel medium works best.

SURFACES

For journaling, basic cardstock or watercolor paper works great, as do index cards. If you wish to make your creations in an actual journal, the ones that open flat are the easiest. Don't worry if the pages are ruled or thin; you can coat the pages with gesso, and they become white and stiff. Handmade Watermark Bindery journals are the perfect paper thickness for sketching and collage, and you get to customize your cover. We like Bare Books journals too, which are inexpensive and look like books. Really, any book can become a journal, with a little glue and gesso. Buy old books at garage sales and thrift stores, and alter those.

Visual journaling allows us to convey our lives in color, texture and pattern—without expensive materials. Our words and art play off each other, joining to represent people and events. It's easy to begin "seeing" your world as a collection of colors, once you look for them.

I AM ART

Start TODAY.
This is the beginning of
something GREAT.

I AM ART. Say it loud and say it strong. You *are* art—right here and now. You do not have to do anything to be "artistic," or learn anything special to be quotable. You are a living, breathing, perfect example of art. You are color, light, form, words, song, sound . . . You are a unique, ever-growing, ever-changing masterpiece. Your visual chronicles of *YOU*, as art, express your colors, your dialogue, your character, your plot, the people, shapes, textures and geometry of your world. Your visual journals are your true offering, presenting the multidimensional art that is uniquely you.

Too often, wonderful artists get bogged down in the fear that they are not "artists." Powerful writers wonder, "What have *I* got to say?" Creative people stop themselves from creating, strangled by *can'ts, don'ts, shouldn'ts* and *better nots*. We are needlessly intimidated by others' evocative artwork, groaning, "Looks great. Wish *I* could do it . . ."

We *can* do it, without prior art training, without being a "journalist." You might be thinking, "Easy for you to say. You *are* an *ARTIST!*" Well, Karen is not; she's a working mom with a left-brain, logical mind and constantly needy young children. The only difference between Karen and you may be that Karen has an artist-sister encouraging (OK, nagging) her to express herself artistically. Now, *you* have two "sisters" encouraging and nagging *YOU*. More than nagging you, we're going to show you: Artistic expression is easy for *you* to do, and fun as all get-out, too! (As in, *get out* your aggressions, *get out* your giggles, *get out* your secrets—get it?)

With paint and words, decorative paper and ticket stubs, rubber stamps and stencils, we can create meaningful, provocative, humorous, unexpected glimpses into our lives. Your journals are safe havens where everyone gets your jokes and you don't have to worry about being grammatically, politically or socially correct. You can make crooked lines. You can let your true colors flow! You can let your imaginary colors reign! Let your sense of humor, your edgy views and your pretty, feminine side coexist (even if you are a man). Get lost in the artful expression of *YOU*; that is where you will find the real "art." Push any useless fears aside and boldly *BE!*

A picture may be worth a thousand words, but a color is worth a thousand words, a thousand people, a thousand emotions, a thousand sounds . . . Whether we consciously realize it or not, we all associate certain colors with moods, sounds, tastes, people, places—almost everything.

Color Your Life   Literally drawing on this colorful resource, you can use colors to represent images and events and to stimulate feelings and memories. Gathering the colors of your past, present and possible future makes visual journaling more "true" to the experience you want to express.

No doubt since our ancestors journaled on their cave walls, people have expressed theories about the meaning of different colors. Certain colors have grown to hold symbolic meanings through their use over the centuries. When Neil Diamond sings a "Song Sung Blue," or when Picasso painted in his Blue Period, we know they were sad. When you look at the world through rose-colored glasses and have a rosy disposition, you are optimistic and cheerful. Tying a yellow ribbon 'round the old oak tree signifies hope, forgiveness, friendship; yellow roses mean friendship. In Russia, red symbolizes beauty; in ancient Rome, it signified battle; in China, red is the color of good luck; in South Africa, red is the color of mourning.

Following are common associations for a range of colors. As you select colors for your journal pages, feel free to use these or turn them upside down!

RED: *Anger, Heat, Love, Fire, "Stop"*
PURPLE: *Passion, Royalty, Wealth, Whimsy*
BLUE: *Water, Sky, Calm, Masculine, Wisdom, Trust*
GREEN: *Nature, Growth, Jealousy, "Go"*
YELLOW: *Cheer, Sun, Warm, Playful, "Caution"*
PINK: *Childhood, Innocence, Feminine, Calm, Daybreak or Sunset*

HAVE NO FEAR!

Color is your friend! The easiest way to jazz up your journal entries is with color. Using color is also the easiest way to create mood, convey emotion and even "make noise."

What colors do you associate with being happy, calm, nervous, annoyed, sad or angry? What color is your best friend? Your boss? Your mother? Your dog? Your favorite cookie? Your tenth birthday? Your dream vacation? Your Personal Palette will be a reference booklet for your life, containing the colors, shapes and textures surrounding you. By creating a Personal Palette, you will have a ready tool to trigger feelings, memories, hopes and images. You will have at your fingertips the colors that symbolize your present, past and imaginary worlds, ready to inspire journal entries and spur-of-the-moment tag art.

personal palette

SIMPLE SUPPLIES

your list of people, emotions, and places, and corresponding colors/patterns for each (*see below*) • paper punch • glue stick • shipping tags • pen • paint swatches (paper samples from a paint or home improvement store) • scissors • computer-generated text or label maker to use for a title • screw post

As you create your personal palette, you cannot help but smile at the associations you make with certain colors, patterns and textures. Start with a person, someone important in your life: What colors come to mind when you imagine this person? Write the person's name on a scratch paper, and write those colors next to the name. Do this for a few people you know will appear in your journal pages—for better or worse! Linda, for example, is definitely a deep red. Karen is a Naples yellow. Our friend Cheryl can be expressed only with a Louis Vuitton logo, because she wouldn't be caught dead or alive in anything but. Our Nana is a checked tablecloth, as she was always ready for a picnic.

Next, jot down some emotions (positive and negative) and their matching colors or patterns. Do the same for key places or activities in your days. Your list might include parents, siblings, spouse or partner, children, boss, best friends, home, school, work, favorite coffee shop, most embarrassing moment, beloved pets, sports, anger, hunger, love, joy, sadness, excitement, etc. With your list ready, let's begin your Personal Palette.

PERSONAL PALETTE

Using the paper punch, punch out the colors you have written on your list. Glue the punched paper(s) to your tag, creating one tag for each person, mood or event.

On each tag, write the name of the person, mood or event that belongs with each color.

Cut out the cover and use a hole punch to make a hole in the top of the tag.

Create a cover for your palette by tracing the shape of your tag on a paint swatch.

Cut out computer-generated text to title your Personal Palette. Glue on your title, and assemble all the tags with a screw post. Admire your work, preferably while eating a little cookie.

Lee and Tod Tags

Our brothers, Lee and Tod, are in our thoughts and journals a lot. Lee was a writer before he could walk, so we "see" him as words, in black-and-white. His color is blue, like his eyes and the color he often wears.

Tod's colors are red, for the laughter and joy he evokes, and brown, for the peanut butter on his shoulder.

Nana and Calm Tags

When Nana isn't baking, she is in her garden, so flowers represent her, together with a cheerful yellow.

The feeling of calm, to us, is a soothing minty-fresh green, or a neutral cream, or an airy blue. If we had a wrapper from a Mint Aero candy bar from England, we'd have stuck it on too!

Adventure and Refreshed Tags

We feel adventurous as we trek through the hills of Killarney, Ireland, lost and probably trespassing. Our colors for adventure are those of the blue sky and green grasses we have crossed.

"Refreshed" colors are clean and bright, energetic and ready for another hike with the sheep; to us, that's lime green and bright yellow.

15

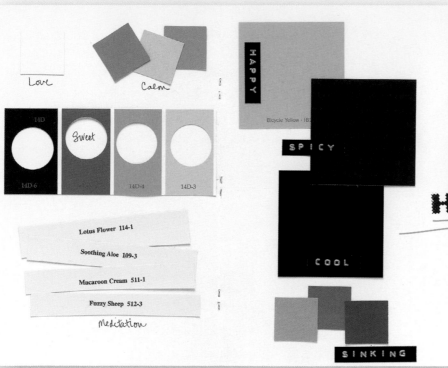

HAVE NO FEAR!

Make a Personal Palette book if you prefer! Take two 8½"x 11" (22cm x 28cm) pieces of cardstock, and fold them in half, placing one piece inside the other. Secure the pages with staples or sew them together. Voilà! A book is born. Decorate the pages with the punched paint swatches, and label them as we did the tags. You can organize the pages by subject or family, if you like.

We have the most fun "painting" people. People often wind up being "painted" the color of their dominant moods or emotions (bossy people, for us, are usually red or orange, and docile people are often pastel blue or pink, for example), or the color of the clothes they most often wear, or the color of the emotions they bring out in us, the artists. Boring people might be gray, even if they dress vibrantly! You get to choose how to build your Personal Palette: The only rule is to be true to yourself. How do you know if you got the "right" color for someone? If it feels right to you, it is right. However, that won't stop Linda from arguing with the person who told her *she* was purple.

You can keep a running list of Personal Palette subjects on a notepad, adding to it over a few days or over a lifetime. Begin the Personal Palette project with whatever strikes you on that day, and then add to it, making your Personal Palette grow with your ideas. This evolving palette is the color map of your life. Refer to it while you create journal pages, as a guide and quick reminder to help you select colors and to inspire ideas and images.

Start TODAY.

This is the beginning of something **GREAT.** Travel. Art. US. what could be better? I HAVE been sitting here all day making the Magic. *It WORKS*

I FEEL LIKE ___

Start Today

Can you see Karen in this journal page? She is here: She's the yellow and orange background! I made this journal page the day we started our Web site (www.sistersonsojourn.com). We were so excited and full of ideas, I had no time to make a neat "book" page. I wrote my thoughts on note paper and glued them to a prepainted background, ready-made with "Karen" colors.— Linda

No Passport

The colors of our favorite countries are well-worn sections of our Personal Palettes! Norway's sky is bluer than its fjords . . . Spicy reds fill the streets of Singapore . . . . Greens of every hue roll across the Welsh countryside. Here, I had a lot to say, so I used a two-page spread and highlighted my words with a simple color wash on the left side. On the right page, I painted the colors that represent three of my favorite destinations.—Linda

NO PASSPORT

This area seems so colorless and bland. No gothic churches, no fjords, no lush gardens, no waterfalls or babbling rivers running through town. My daydreams will be of those things. I will bathe the house in rich colors to remind me of my journey. Walking into the kitchen will be like walking in the Piazza San Marco. The hall bathroom will be Florence! And, our bedroom Chelsea Blue Singapore for the living room and Norway in the loft. I'll never want to leave home!

REQUIRED

Scandinavia

Asia

Wales

Celebrate life

THE SPARK OF BEING gotten

Gotten

Our childhood summers were spent with our Nana, in a big, happy house full of yellow and orange, that smelled like toasted strawberry Pop-Tarts. We now associate yellow, red and orange with feeling full and cheerful. However, if your Nana belittled you throughout her moldy-smelling yellow house, you may feel quite differently. The red heart and the yellow background convey my inner celebration!—Linda

17

A Place to Heal

We found this bench surrounded by purple flowers on a small side street with a view of the city center. I want to sit here all day and just absorb everything and write it all down before I forget. It is hard to write while eating an ice cream bar and watching life go by. It must be noon, the church bells are calling out to us. I love this bench.

We walked and walked and kept seeing the same door in different colors

busy

TIME TO

FEAR BUSTER NO. 1

I HAVE NO TIME

If you love looking at other people's visual journals and dream of the pages you'd make if you "only had the time," we have great news for you: *You have the time!* We are busy girls and don't have hours a day to spend on our journals, and you don't need to, either. Your journals will be spontaneous, energetic and alive if you drop any limiting thoughts about what a "journal" should be, and turn the art you have and are into your journal. With a few fast, easy tricks, you can be ready to journal in no time.

The first trick is to open your mind and your heart. The only things you need to begin visual journaling are an imagination and emotions. People *think* it would take a long time just to start journaling, because they *think* they won't be able to *think* up what to put on that page. So *stop thinking*. Start observing. Start feeling. Start looking at your daily life as if you were visiting a foreign country, delighting in every color and scent, laughing at little mishaps that take you on a new path, stopping to touch cool water in a fountain. As you remember that you are art, and each moment is part of the landscape complementing you, you immediately have plenty to fill a blank page.

Next, your Personal Palette has already made journaling faster and easier. It is a wonderful prompt for times when you feel like creating, but aren't sure what to create. Just flip through your Palette tags and see who, where or what inspires you. And when you know just what you need to say, your Personal Palette helps you say it quickly. You don't need lots of planning time before you actually journal. You won't have to stop to ponder what color to paint the background of your morning, or your welling frustration about remodeling, or your joy in seeing your garden's first blossom: The colors are in front of you, ready to personalize your expression of emotion.

Don't spend hours searching for the "right" journal. Join us as we journal outside the book! Jot your thoughts on shipping tags, sketch impressions on torn pieces of watercolor paper, grab self-stick notes, index cards tucked in your purse, the back of grocery store receipts, shoes—anything. You can glue your journal page into a book later, or simply store loose journal pages in a decorated box. We recommend good sources for the journals we love in our Resources section, even some small enough to take anywhere. Don't get bogged down by choosing a book and thinking you have to schlep it with you everywhere: Journal now, worry about a book later!

Nor do you have to spend days searching for and buying special journaling materials. Use pencils, chalk, ink pens, crayons, permanent markers, simple stencils, watercolor paint, inkpads, acrylic paint, cutouts from magazines, wrapping paper, rubber stamps, glue sticks . . . many, many things you have lying around your house all the time, already. As you skim the samples in this book, notice the variety of media used. Some pages use only decorative paper and handwriting; some use only lettering and rubbed-on ink; some use photos embellished with a bit of paint. Whatever you have at home now, turn it into an artful extension of you! (When you do have the time, let's meet up at the craft store for a shopping spree!)

Finally, you do not have to set aside journaling time in your day. We keep basic journaling materials in easy reach, and then we can snatch 15 minutes to chronicle how we spilled all the cookie batter on our new suede shoes. Or we include journaling among our multitasking options: Journaling can be done while watching TV, talking on the phone, helping kids with homework, and waiting at baseball practices, to name just a few options.

"Finding" time is particularly easy when you have some pieces for journaling ready all the time, and then you can add to them, or become inspired by them, later on. The easiest way to get a quick start on journaling is to have some backgrounds already made. Using your Personal Palette as a guide, make some backgrounds suited to emotions, people and places you know will be useful in the weeks to come.

For example, if blue is your color for meditation, paint a light blue wash over a piece of paper or a journal page, in anticipation of an entry about meditating. If you've been angry at your new boss, and red is your color for anger, paint a background with shades of red. If gingham checks remind you of your grandmother, use some decorative paper to cover a journal page, or the page border, and you may later be inspired to journal about a favorite memory with your grandmother. If Ferris wheels make you giggle, use a "happy" color wash and a rubber stamp of a Ferris wheel on one of your pages. Paint or ink some tags to carry in your day planner for spontaneous journaling!

HAVE NO FEAR!

Mix colors and textures in your background—play! Evoke different moods and memories with movement and shading. It's fun to take a large piece of paper and paint several overlapping or splattered colors on it, then randomly tear the paper into smaller pieces for journaling later.

creating pre-painted backgrounds

SIMPLE SUPPLIES

Personal Palette (see page 13) to conjure the colors of the people, places, emotions and relationships surrounding you • watercolor paper, index cards, a journal or any surface of your choice • gesso • flat brushes • acrylic paint • acrylic glazing medium • palette or disposable plate for paints • paper towels • cosmetic sponges • dye- or pigment-based inkpads

HAVE NO FEAR!

If you fear the kids knocking paint all over the carpet while you "multitask," invest a few dollars in some dye- or pigment-based inkpads to use for your backgrounds. It is so easy to make cool backgrounds with Petal Points or Paint-Box inkpads, and they last a long time. You can make marbled, aged and sponged effects without dripping a bit.

1

Paint your page with a thin layer of gesso and let it dry.

2

Mix equal parts of paint and glazing medium on your palette.

Paint the glaze mixture all over your page.
Be generous. Don't let it dry yet!

Real fast now, rub off some of the paint with a paper towel.
Now you can let it dry.

If desired, you can now add another color to your page. You might want to use a different shade of the same color, or a contrasting color.

Add shading and shadows with ink! Dab a cosmetic sponge on an inkpad, then sponge the ink around the edges of your painted page.

simple ways to add texture and lettering

A single word paired with the right colors makes a huge impact. Several ways exist to help your words "speak." Rubber stamp alphabets are easy to use and make a bold impact, but we also like using rub-on lettering and vinyl stick-on letters.

Still need some other lettering ideas? Simple handwriting is great, unique to you and inserts you in your journal page immediately. Letters from friends or family do the same, capturing these people through their writing. Cutting out letters from a magazine can create an edgy feel, or for a "blast from the past," have fun with a Dymo labeler!

Your computer is your fastest lettering source, and free fonts, even free handwriting-style fonts, are available on the Internet. We each had our handwriting made into a font so we could print it out (and spell-check it!).

SIMPLE SUPPLIES

watercolor paper, or any surface of your choice • dye- or pigment-based inkpad (light-colored) • cosmetic sponges • rubber stamps (including alphabet stamps) • photo • acrylic paint • palette or disposable plate for paints • glazing medium • rub-on letter sheet • stylus • vinyl letter sheet

USING RUBBER STAMPS

1

Dab a cosmetic sponge on an inkpad, then rub the sponge gently over your page to create a mottled background texture. Re-ink your sponge as needed.

2

Using a light-colored inkpad, ink your rubber stamp. Randomly stamp the image on your page, over the mottled background. *Lovely.*

3

Before stamping your words, lay the stamps on the page and see if they fit. It's OK if they don't. But, if you want the whole word, check first. Stamp your letters with dark ink so they show up on the textured background.

1

Mix equal parts paint and glazing medium. Paint the white areas of your photo. Don't let it dry yet.

2

While the glaze mixture is still wet, dab the painted area of your photo a few times with a cosmetic sponge to mute the colors. OK, now you can let it dry.

HAVE
NO FEAR!

When in doubt, MAKE IT BIG. Use bigger lettering and make a bold statement!

3

Place the rub-on letter sheet where you want your words to begin. Using the stylus, rub carefully over each letter of your word to transfer it to the page.

4

To use stick-on letters, remove the vinyl letters from the backing sheet, and place them on your page. Think carefully first, because you cannot peel them off and restick them. (Um, we know this from experience.)

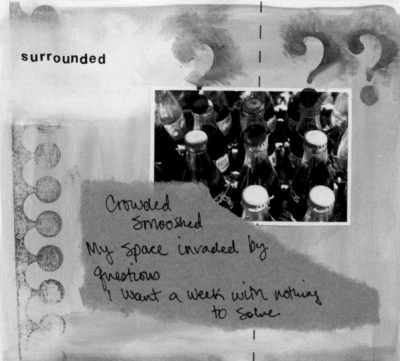

Surrounded

I first scrawled my feelings of "crowded and smooshed" on a scrap of paper torn from a grocery bag! Later, I combined it with a picture of "crowded" bottles, a stamped shape that mimicked the bottle shapes, and rubber-stamped question marks. I used rub-on letters over white paint for the overriding emotion: "surrounded". I think the rub-on letters look jostled, as I felt. By allowing my stamping to smear a bit, I accented the feeling of agitation.—Linda

A Place to Heal

Ahhhhhh. I say that every time I look at this page! Part of me is still sitting on this lovely bench in England, healed. I wrote about our perfect afternoon in a handwriting font on my computer, printed it out, and glued it into my journal. I printed out a picture of the bench in black and white, then I lightly painted purple and brown accents on the picture. I glued it in my journal and added touches of paint near the "title," as well.—Linda

We walked and walked and kept seeing the same door in different colors.

A Place to Heal

We found this bench surrounded by purp[le] flowers on a small side street with a vie[w] the city center. I want to sit here all d[ay] and just absorb everything and write it down before I forget. It is hard to write while eating an ice cream bar and watching life go by. It must be noon, the church bells are calling out to us. I love th[e] bench.

I CAN'T WRITE

With premade colorful backgrounds, you no longer have "scary" white paper staring at you, daring you to mar its pristine surface. If a nay-saying voice in your head nevertheless wails, "But I can't write!", calmly respond, "No problemo." First, you can write; and second, you don't have to be "a writer." Your journal is like holding up a mirror to you: Everything it shows you is some aspect of you, reflected. A glimpse is as valuable as a full-length, and magnifications are often the most interesting!

Journal writing is easy because it is something you do for yourself. If you want to let people read it, see into your soul and enjoy your amazing art, great, but create journals for *YOU*. And since you are writing and creating art for yourself, keep in mind as you write, paint, collage and stamp that you already know the characters and destinations (real or imaginary) in your journal pages. You do not need to explain who everyone is in relation to you. You already know that. Write as if you are talking to yourself. Don't get muddled in details; don't feel you have to justify how you portray anyone or any idea. If you decide to let people into your secret journal world and they have questions about who is who, they will ask. And then you will choose how to answer.

Journals, in whatever form, capture what all of your senses have perceived, translate those images, and present them as only you can. Be aware of what you see, hear, smell, touch, taste and feel. As you go about your day, ask yourself, "What color is the sound of this Metro train? What word describes my fear of being late again?" Your increased awareness will help words flow for journaling. Keep a little notepad with you, and write ideas, words or descriptions as they pop into your head. You may think you will later remember your brilliant ideas; trust us on this and *write them down!*

Thinking Out Loud

Journaling is almost like leaving a tape recorder on in your head all day. To the sounds of the cities, shops, families, friends and workplaces you visit on your daily sojourns, add what you hear in your lovely head. Think of your inner dialogue as almost a sixth sense, usually truer than whatever sounds everyone else can hear. Journals are visual media, but you can convey sounds through color and words, and you will have a blast doing it!

We all have internal conversations while we do everyday, typical things. The voice in your head that notices, then exclaims, *"Only one cashier, and twelve people in line?"* is the one you want to listen to when writing your journal entries. That voice is the spontaneous, unedited *you* that makes for wildly entertaining and moving journals. That voice also leads to self-discovery and solutions. Start paying attention to the running commentary "upstairs" and you may be surprised by your wisdom, insight and creativity.

When people nevertheless feel "writer's block," they mean one of two things: Either they feel blocked because they have too, too much to say, or they feel blocked because they have nothing to say. Luckily, the solution to both problems is the same: focus!

By using colors from your Personal Palette, mixed with your choice of pictures, papers or photos (or none) and a few words, you can easily create great visual journals. Whether you run into block number one (your brain is crammed fuller than Linda's ephemera boxes) or block number two (your mind is as empty as a candy wrapper on Karen's birthday), pick *one thing* to focus on, and journal about that.

"But what *one* thing?" you ask. Easy. Pick *one* person, or *one* place, or *one* thing. Write about the person who made you late, or the place where the craziness occurred, or the thing that went haywire because you were late (not that Karen is ever late). Often, details are unnecessary. Your words can be simply: *"GOING HAYWIRE."* That is the memorable "thing" that happened today. You do not have to explain what went haywire or where. Narrow your focus, and you say more. Use a few well-chosen words. In fact, challenge yourself to use no more than ten. Few of our journal pages have more than ten words, and some of our favorites have less. Now, tell us, who can't write ten little words?

28

HAVE NO FEAR!

Visual journaling is a great way to get out anger and frustration—more fun than therapy, and a heck of a lot cheaper! If you are worried that someone will see that you journaled about her, be sneaky: Create a symbol for that person and she will never know you have journaled about her! Your gossipy neighbor could be the smashed red telephone in your "Moving On" journal entry . . .

Once prompted, we can all be insightful writers. You can choose from many focal points. Another easy way to focus your thoughts and choose your words is to *pick one sense.* What did you *see, hear, taste, smell, touch* or *intuit?* Focus on just one sense to express on

Finding a Focus

your tag or page. If you see roses today and they remind you of your wedding, you could do this: Cut out pictures of roses, glue them on a background pre-painted with your love or happy colors, and write on that page something simple, like: "In bloom at my wedding." It will be beautiful. Linda did it (see page 61) and so can you! You can also depict the same day or incident from different perspectives by making several pages focusing on different senses. What you hear may yield a completely different image than what you feel or see!

HAVE NO FEAR!

If you want to journal six tags about the same day, by all means, DO SIX! Start with one sense (what you "saw," perhaps), and you will have no problem "writing"!

Here are three easy prompts to remember: Pick *one noun* or *one verb* or *one adjective.* Write about what you did (sweating, dreaming, swimming, eating), or the size of something (too big to handle!), or the feel of something (comfy), or the "thing itself" (the lost dog, the bad haircut, the annoying underwear . . . yes, *all* subjects that we, ourselves have written about!).

You can also just break your day into bite-size morsels, by choosing one time frame: morning, noon or night. Focus on one-third of your day to journal about. For example, if you laughed through lunch because your friend Judy forgot to meet you and the girls for a picnic, make a quick page with decorative paper and a few words (see page 98 for an example). Or if your day was too hectic, capture the big, crazy picture and skip the details.

If you still feel blocked, interview yourself. Ask: "What funny thing happened today?" "What sad thing happened today?" "What annoying thing happened today?" "What did I learn today?" "Who did I meet today?" "What was my best birthday party ever?" You are a star! If you had to find something to discuss on a talk show for 15 minutes, you could. So journal about it!

mini prompt journal

HAVE NO FEAR!

Make your prompts your own! It's OK if no one else understands them. One of Karen's favorite prompts is "Psycho Spots." SHE knows what that means, and that's all that matters.

"GET GOING!" That's what a good writing and art prompt will shout to you, encouraging you to spill some color, splash on words, spin an image and speak your mind! We often come up with prompts as we talk to each other. One of us will say, "Oh, you must journal about that!" and a prompt is born. "Memory Tripping" is one of our favorite prompts. As we were driving to teach a workshop and laughing over funny memories from our childhood, we realized we have so many memories we want to journal about! So we scrawled "memory tripping" on a notepad full of prompt ideas, and made a prompt tag later.

Your Mini Prompt Journal is a companion to your Personal Palette. Use the colors from your Personal Palette to create a portable journal of personalized prompts—ideas to inspire and get you going. You can use some of the same simple prompts we love, or create completely different ones. We add to our Mini Prompt Journal often, as new "must journal that!" ideas hit us. We hate to see a great idea go to waste!

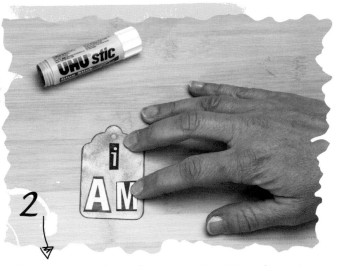

Rub ink on the surface of one tag with a cosmetic sponge, creating a mottled background. Using a Petal Point or Cat's Eye inkpad, rub a contrasting ink color on the edges of the tag to add definition.

Cut out words or letters from a magazine. Using glue stick, adhere the lettering to your tag to create prompts for your journal entries and get you going!

Create another prompt, by tracing the tag shape onto decorative paper. Cut out the paper and then glue it onto a tag. Punch a hole in the top of the tag.

Write your prompt in computer-generated text and glue it to the tag. When you have made several prompt tags, assemble them with a screw post or brad.

Good Journey

This page was inspired by the "Roads Traveled" prompt tag. We arrived at this empty train station after a month of exploring England. The calm of this early morning lull allowed us to reflect on our good journey. I used a black-and-white photo, handwritten text and a postage stamp. Looking at this journal page calms me and reminds me of so many wonderful roads we sisters have traveled.—*Linda*

Flood's Over

Our "What's So Funny" prompt tag inspires many journal pages, some of which we probably should keep to ourselves! Funny thoughts and making fun can come across in cartoon-like journal pages. Doodles are just plain funny, and fun to do. Watercolors bring a childlike feel to this page, too. As I looked in the mirror one morning at my shrunken pants, I couldn't pass up this observation!—*Linda*

Wine and Art

One picture or one word often sends me "flying" back in time, so I can actually hear, smell and feel a memory. A long weekend of art making, wine tasting and venting with friends is one of my best memories. Both the wine and the whine made our art better, but the crème brûlée helped the most! We three friends (represented by three different colored bottles) had the best time! This page was prompted by my "Memory Tripping" prompt tag.—Linda

Get More Sleep

While the blue paint was still wet on this page, I scraped some off with the end of my paintbrush to make the pattern of a cozy quilt. It's funny for how many years I tried to avoid the cruelty of having to sleep, only to wish that I could do so now. I created this page after glancing at my "Wishes" prompt tag, and I used black vinyl letters and red Dymo labeling, plus stenciled gold stars to symbolize sweet dreaming.—Linda

Do, Doing . . . Done?

Never-ending "to-do" lists and my "Woe is Me" prompt tag inspired this page. I feel like I am always either needing to do or in the midst of doing, but never DONE! The colored spiral matched the feeling of going a long way to get nowhere. These vibrant, busy colors perfectly capture the frantic mood.—Karen

Powerful Prompts

I Am . . .	Wishes	Hearing Things
What's So Funny?	Who Said That?	Bor-ing!
Self-Portrait	Uh-oh . . .	Routines
Roads Traveled	Who? What? Where?	Morning, Noon, Night
Woe Is Me!	Work	Mmmm-mmm, Good!
Memory Tripping	That Pushes My Buttons!	That Made My Day!

The first trick to cracking "journaler's block" is to zoom in. These prompt ideas help us pick an image or a few words to get us going. Make your portable Prompt Journal with prompts that get your mind racing, and you will start to look at your days differently. You'll see broken pipes, or a pen pal's letter, as potential journal pages; you'll look at your breakfast plate and run to journal about your silly breakfast "routines." Now, when we sit in the dentist's office, flipping through magazines, we look more at words and fonts than at who's had a nose job. We see the word "scandal!" and think, "Hey, a new prompt! Scandals!" We see a picture of a dandelion and think, "That would be perfect for a 'Wishes' page!" Then, uh, we tear out the picture and hope no one notices . . .

Many of our prompts spring from a desire to explore our interior worlds. Knowing what makes you tick is essential; it is also . . . *art!* We all have "buttons" that get pushed, triggering anger, frustration, joy, rage—the gamut of emotions. Recognizing and capturing our "buttons" not only helps us know ourselves, it also gives us back to ourselves, somehow disempowering the button, it seems. This next project causes more spontaneous emotion than any other we do in our workshops, so be warned: Your family or roommates may think you have gone nuts as your sinister laugh erupts from your room. It is hysterical to show others your "buttons" and watch their eyes widen in complete understanding . . . or abject horror.

"that pushes my buttons" journal

SIMPLE SUPPLIES

3" × 5" (8cm × 13cm) spiral-bound index cards • gesso • flat brush • acrylic paint of your choice • scissors • junk mail • glue stick • alphabet stamps • black inkpad • gel medium • buttons • decorative paper • label maker

When doing "buttons" pages, we've found that the second trick to overcome "journaler's block" is to be brief: The Journal Police won't ticket you for using more than ten words, but by aiming for ten, you surely won't feel the intimidation of writer's block! Your Personal Palette colors and any images will be worth many words, so you do not need a lot of words to make your point.

Sometimes, you will want to use more words, when you have a longer story to tell or when the words are the focal point of your entry. In that case, you can use a simple color wash as a background to highlight your words,

without competing with them for attention. You might also want to try a two-page spread, with words on one page and images on another. (See page 17 for a sample journal entry with lots of writing.)

When you know what words you want to use, don't bury them! Be equally brief with your color choices: Pick no more than three colors, and accent with black and white. Three colors usually are plenty to convey your thoughts, images and feelings and are enough to create a whole landscape. Three colors will not hide your words, either. Most important, who can be intimidated by three little colors?

Cover two facing index cards in the spiral-bound "journal" with gesso.

After the gesso has dried, apply a solid wash of color to both pages, adding white over the color to soften it, if you like.

Cut out text and postage from junk mail. Adhere them to the left page with the glue stick.

On the right page, stamp your words, using alphabet stamps and black ink.

Using gel medium, attach your button beneath the words.

"THAT PUSHES MY BUTTONS" COVER

Trim decorative paper to 4" × 5" (10 cm × 13 cm). Using glue stick, adhere the paper to the front of the journal. Notch out the corners with scissors.

Apply glue stick to the flaps of paper, then fold them to the inside of the cover and burnish them down with your fingers.

Cut a piece of paper to 2¾" × 4½" (7cm × 11cm) and glue it to the inside of the journal.

Embellish the cover with a title, using a label maker.

HAVE NO FEAR!

Make a tag journal instead if you want! You can get a bound tag journal at a craft store, and glue buttons and papers right in it. Find images for your button pages on royalty-free clip art Web sites, or use your own photos. Then vent about whatever pushes your buttons!

Don't Push My Buttons

This tag journal is perfect for taking on my business trips. I bring a travel kit of journaling supplies, and then I can memorialize every annoyance, from too-small hotel towels to bad Internet connections. —Karen

39

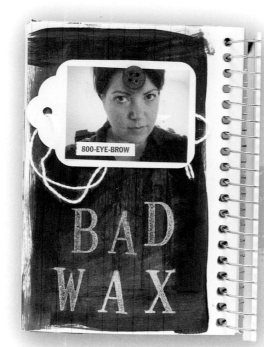

Bad Wax

Red is my angry color, and nothing makes me madder than a bad eyebrow wax. I liberally applied anger to this page and added an annoyed-looking picture of myself, bad wax and all. The words are stamped with white ink, like melty wax. The button is red too and is placed just right to emphasize the offending area.—Linda

Dish Gloves

Green is my irritated color, and pink is my domestic diva color. When the two collide, watch out! I painted vibrant green on both pages, and when the left page was dry, I painted a light coat of pink over the center of the green. I glued down my glove image and buttons, then rubber-stamped the words. This is a four-button page, I was so annoyed.—Linda

Kaboom

I am a magnet for uninsured motorists. Many a blue-skied, sunny, Southern California day has been ruined for me by some road warrior without insurance. The skies then turn muddy and dark as my red anger grows, because I know full well the driver will be too busy at rehab to work and pay for my car repairs. I used handwriting and cutout text for my wording.—Linda

Juicy Gossip

This is a HAPPY button! Circles represent life energy to me, and hot pink is my color for wicked fun. The overall effect of this image is an irresistible, juicy berry. I created the circles by placing circle stickers randomly on the page, then painting pink over them. When the paint was dry, I removed the stickers. I then glued on the words and a button.—Linda

GET GOING:

"I Am..." Journal

Journals traditionally are a place for self-discovery and revelation. We like to use our visual journals for self-creation, as well, so we can open the pages of who we are, who we've been and who we are becoming. None of the pages has to be true. That's half the fun. We loved playing make-believe as kids, and, in our journals, we still can! When we were kids, we created with abandon, turning mistakes into flowers and making every corner a smiling sun. We never hesitated as our hands neared the paper, because it was OK if the ink smeared or the line was crooked. The point was telling our story, showing our vision, and being ourselves.

Now, we have several prompts that help us loosen up and feel like fearless kids again. These prompts give us tons of ideas, and let us see or show different parts of ourselves. One prompt that always inspires us is completing the sentence "I am . . ." It seems we find a new way to complete that sentence every day. Ask yourself who you are within your family, at work, in your friendships, as a child, as a parent, when you play sports, or while you drive. Travel to your past: Think, "I am ten years old," and see who you are then. Or look into the future, imagine retirement, and journal what that looks like.

Honestly chronicle your quirks. Everybody else is laughing at them, so you may as well join in. When you create a journal page dedicated to your mastery of the deviled egg, or your obsession over misplaced apostrophes, you truly accept and celebrate who you are. Use the "I Am . . ." prompt to organize your thoughts and feelings, too. When we've been mulling over something for a while, it often helps to express our current feelings through art. Having to complete that sentence forces you to be mindful, to quiet competing voices and find the one that is yours.

Start TODAY
This is the beginning of
something GREAT.
Travel. Art. Us. what

AFRAID OF THE DEEP END

Afraid of the Deep End

People always ask why I sit in the shade, at the edge of the pool. Year after year, I answer the same thing: I am afraid of the deep end. I do not make excuses; I do not try to explain. This is simple, and it is not changing. These waves are stenciled in pool-water blue, and the words are stamped in black. The page is stark, like the silence that follows my answer. —Linda

Waiting for a New Day

This is one of my favorite photos. I imagine myself sitting upon this bench, planning and plotting all sorts of adventures. The original photo is in color, but I like the mystery of black-and-white. Sky blue paint flows like rolling clouds above the bench, signaling that a new day IS coming . . . —Linda

WAITING FOR A NEW day

Good at Silly Hair

Whether it's transforming children into Silly Hair Day Contest contenders or teens into punk rockers, I am the go-to gal for hair creations. I used glue-type gel, colored mousse—oops, wrong how-to. The purple pinstriped paper accents the high hair in this Polaroid photo, and no silly hairdo is complete without a big, puffy bow! I used my handwriting on the picture.—Karen

Good at silly hair

Uh oh.

NOT GOOD at CATCHING things

Not Good at Catching Things

I can't catch a football, and I can't draw a football, but I can cut out a picture of one speeding toward my head, as has happened so many times in real life. The exaggerated scale of the football compared to my head matches my perceptions and helps me laugh at my quirks. The girly flowers are stamped in white, and I used rub-on letters.—Linda

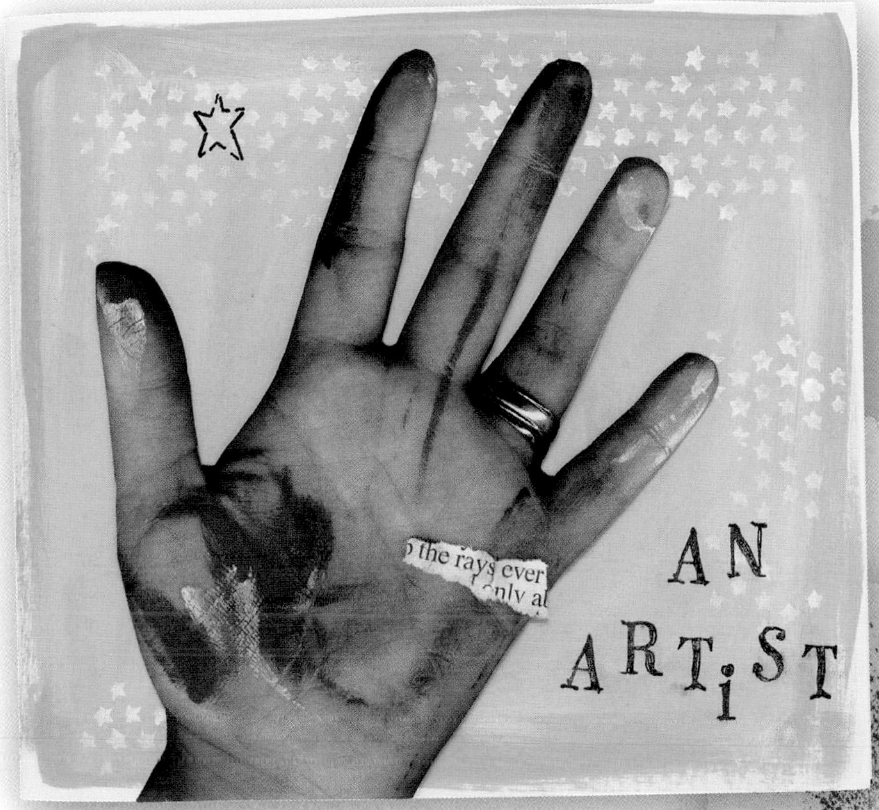

An Artist

The on-the-job hazard of being an artist is that you never have clean hands or nice nails; something is always stuck on you somewhere! Five minutes into one of my days, I put my hand on the copy machine and copied it. I cut it out and glued it on my background, painted happy yellow. I stamped my title in black and stamped a star near the top.—*Linda*

AN ARTiST

the rays ever only at

A Little Sister, Number 3

No matter what else I am, I will always be a little sister, the third one, one of "the kids." I randomly splattered paint on this page to match the colors of the beach where we played as kids. I glued on the picture, then rubber-stamped the number 3, overlapping the photo and the words beneath it.—*Linda*

NO. 3

A LITTLE SISTER

always
getting
LOST

You'd think that since I get lost so much, I'd be the one who is late all the time . . . I love maps, and used this one as a coloring book to make my journal page. Using the markings on the map, I painted light green, dark green, then purple in different areas of the Santa Clarita Valley in Southern California. The dark purple line is my oft-traveled path; the red stamped X is where I somehow wind up. I used rub-on and vinyl sticker lettering. —*Linda*

Keeping an Open Mind

An open window and an open mind have a lot in common: Things flow freely in and out of both. The base of this page is simply decorative paper. I added a splash of blue paint near the top and accented with a small window and rub-on lettering. The text beneath the window is rubber-stamped. —*Linda*

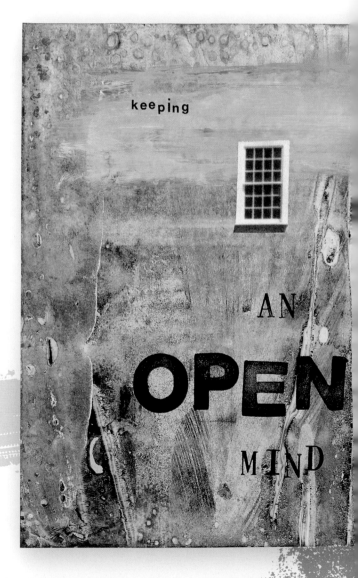

keeping
AN
OPEN
MIND

GET GOING:
Wishes Journal

We've all played the game "If you had three wishes . . ." It's still fun to play. Wishing keeps us in touch with our childlike, creative spirits. When we have time to journal, or when we use a portable journaling kit on the run, we open our little notepad of ideas and our Prompt Journal, and we zoom right in on a topic for the moment. We often gravitate to our "Wishes" prompt. Maybe that's because we often wish to be somewhere else, or to be better at being right where we are.

Our Wishes pages reflect reactions to what is going on around or within our lives: I wish it was sunny instead of raining. I wish I could fit in those pants. I wish I was in Norway. I wish I didn't have varicose veins on my ankles. I wish I had ankles. I wish the employees could be paid more. Our Wishes journal pages also can take us into the past or future. By "wishing," we can rewrite and repaint embarrassing or painful memories, creating alternate pasts in which they never occurred. Our futures likewise speak to us in expressive colors, with simple, effective words that call us to action. Our Wishes pages inspire us to capture our dreams, figuratively and literally.

Whether you wish for real or wish pure fantasies, bring them all to life in your journal pages. Use your Personal Palette to ground your wishes in meaningful colors and patterns. Notice in these samples how varied the styles can be with wishes; that's one reason they are so much fun to do. You can draw a simple ink picture and fill it in with a few watercolors later. Or use some fabric scraps that remind you of a place (or an age) you wish to be; just glue them on your page, and write a few words about your wish. The fabric will convey so much for you. Don't feel like you have to use the words "I wish." The desire will flow through your colors, patterns, images and word choice.

Start TODAY
This is the beginning of
something GREAT.
Travel. Art. US. what

i WISH WE ALL LIVED
on the same street

On the Same Street

As a child, I always thought the four of us kids would grow up to live on the same street. We don't, so it's still a wish I send to the first star at night. Because I've had this wish since childhood, a childlike drawing felt right for it. I drew simple houses and accented them with varied sizes of rubber-stamped lettering.—Linda

Florence

Swirling light fixtures and a swirling Renaissance sky, not to mention swirly pastry tops, are the things I wish for on hectic city days. I created my own background for this cutout of the Florence Duomo, using burnt yellows that conjure up the gilded elements throughout this glorious city. I doodled random shapes and attached a list of possible vacation destinations to the right page.—Linda

Maybe we should just go back to Florence. How did I not notice the cool swirly light fixtures? I want some like that.

who go where they wear dreadlocks

Planning our Escape !!!   DATE 4/3
—Vacation Ideas—
England (scones)
Italy (pasta)
China (rice)
Hawaii (coconut)
New Zealand (?) what do they eat there?

It must've been the jet-lag: I see them clearly NOW. I wonder what else I didn't notice?

Secret Garden

When I saw the gazebo and stone path leading to a secret garden, I knew this house was for us. I painted the top blue, fading into green at the bottom, to suggest the garden. Photos of my blooming flowers and home (now, don't be stalking me!) illustrate my wish-come-true.—
Linda

home

I always wanted a house with a secret garden

I'M JUST NOT ARTISTIC

Do you sabotage yourself by dismissively proclaiming, "I'm just not artistic"? So what? All you have to *be* is alive. Now that you have your Personal Palette, your Prompt Journal fills you with ideas, and we agree you can "write," if you are alive, you can be . . . artful (since you've already disavowed "artistic"). Let's begin with the easiest and least time-consuming way to add some pizzazz (not to be confused with *pizzas*—which would be good, too) to your journals. A little color can make a huge difference!

If you can sign your name, you can add color to your journal. In fact, you can sign your name several times, in colors, just to show yourself how *YOU* can be artistic. You can use colors from your Personal Palette that are right for your mood. Your name will take on new meaning with each color, with each flourish of the pen or brush, and the whole page will artfully mean something to you, depending on what all the colors and flourishes combine to create.

A black-and-white signature speaks too, but it says something totally different. Nothing's wrong with black-and-white if that is what you like, what suits your emotions, or how you feel confident creating. When black-and-white does not match or highlight your experience, that is when you feel you haven't been "artistic." Just by using colors to border your page, or to underline key words, or to circle a phrase, you will express more "artistically."

HAVE NO FEAR!

Don't be stingy with the paint: Squeeze it out and paint it on liberally! SHOW your COLORS!

Simple shapes drawn on the page also add energy and interest. By using geometric figures or a grid layout, you can direct attention to certain words or pictures, or just add more visual appeal to your page. If you want to experiment, try painting different-size squares on a page so that they fill up the page. Think about what colors represent the subject or mood of your entry: perhaps green and blue for outdoors, or dark brown and gold for peanut butter cups. If you want, you can outline your squares in white or black, to offset them from the background. The same thing can be done with circles or triangles. Then, you can write on top of the shapes, or write on a torn piece of paper and glue the paper onto your painted background.

experiments with composition

We all know what great journals look like and how intimidating they can appear. What we *want* to know is what to do when ours are somehow "off," when something is bugging us about a page and we need to fix it and we cannot sleep or stop eating until we do. But **WHAT** to **FIX?** Fear not; the Rule of Thirds comes to the rescue. The Rule of Thirds is a guideline for placing elements on your page so they draw the eye to your focal point, while the elements stay balanced. To follow this easy rule, begin by dividing your page into thirds horizontally and vertically. Lightly draw lines across the page in pencil; two horizontal lines and two vertical lines, forming nine quadrants. (Resist the urge to play tic-tac-toe by yourself!)

Next, ask yourself three questions: "What is my background?" "What is my main point, my focus?" "What elements accent my focus?" You may change your mind about the answers to these questions as you plan your composition, but begin with some ideas you can play with. Balance can begin with your background: Try painting two-thirds of the page a lighter color and one-third a deeper shade. Or, to emphasize where your words will be placed, paint a different shade in the space where two of your grid lines intersect, painting within and just outside one of the nine quadrants. The same idea works with decorative papers. Pick a sheet of paper for the entire background, or add a contrasting paper on one-third. Rubber-stamping is another alternative: Stamp images on the bottom third of the page, and place your text or photo in the top two-thirds of the page.

Now, place your focal point (images or words) within one of the thirds, or near the intersections of the thirds. For example, place a photo so part of it covers a spot where two lines cross. Then, add your accents. You might place your words to the right of your photo, in another spot where horizontal and vertical grid lines cross. Looking at the overall effect, you may push things around a bit before gluing them down. Watch as Linda does just that next, when she plays with composition.

HAVE NO FEAR!

Blank spaces are GOOD. They do not mean you forgot something! Use white space, or colored space, to balance elements or convey an emotion. Just properly size your elements to the page—which leads us back to: When in doubt, go BIG.

EXPERIMENTS WITH COMPOSITION

South East Essex College
of Arts & Technology
Luker Road, Southend-on-Sea Essex SS1 1ND
Tel:(01702) 220400 Fax:(01702) 432320 Minicom: (01702) 220642

1

I begin by placing all elements in the middle of the page.

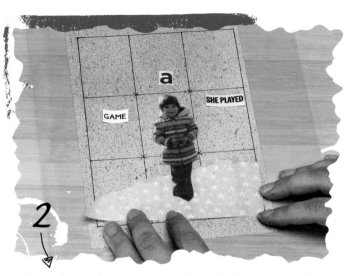

2

I try placing the contrasting color at the bottom, and the words in a halo around that adorable girl. But see how the words appear disjointed?

3

I like the girl on the yellow hill, so I try placing the words together at the bottom. Nope. Too bottom heavy. And it feels like it needs a little kick.

4

Yes! A red ball! I move the girl to the left third, where grid lines intersect. I move the words to the right, where grid lines intersect, and add some height.

5

Finally, I place the ball in the bottom third, on the same vertical grid line as the text. My page is balanced, draws the eye in, and is complete. (Note: Grid lines are for reference only.)

53

Blue

Remember when you had no responsibilities and you could sit in an easy chair all day, listening to music and wallowing in self-pity? Here the chair is front and center, dominating the page. The music plays in the background, in the left third. The thoughts of feeling astray linger beneath the chair in the bottom right. —Linda

There is a Heart

I was feeling particularly prickly this day, yet still vulnerable. My artichokes dutifully marched off the bottom third of the page, while my heart still shone, symbolized by the red circle in the upper left third. The heart is where the top and left thirds intersect; it draws you in. This limited palette focuses your attention. —Linda

SLOW DOWN

TODAY WAS WAY TOO Hectic. I wanted to stop. I wanted TO BREATHE.

O2

Slow Down

This spinning ball of red captures my crazed feelings on a hectic day! The geometric shape is a bold focal point, and my key words, "Slow down", are placed at the intersection of the top and middle thirds of the page. I did not want my other words to detract from the impact of the spinning feeling, so I placed them in the bottom third of the page. Note that it is not important to explain why my day was crazy; a few words were enough. —Linda

As you flip through magazines, you will see that most advertisements follow the Rule of Thirds. The eye-popping portion may be in the bottom third of the advertisement, with sky, stars and some words in the upper two-thirds. Or the right two-thirds may feature a photo of a kissing couple, while the left third is black, with white words describing the engagement ring. Most long articles also follow the Rule of Thirds. Articles with pictures are a great inspiration because they show words combined with images on a page. Instead of copying the outfits on models, start copying the look of the magazine page itself. When you see a magazine layout you love, copy it!

Journal pages send a strong, clear message with straight lines or centered images. You are not "violating" the Rule of Thirds by centering a picture or some large words, and you will see some pages where we have done just that. When you want a central image, or when words are your focal point, use the Rule of Thirds to help you place other elements on the page, or to decide how to paint or design your background. With a photo centered on the page, your words can dance around it, beginning in the upper left or lower right thirds of the page. If words fill the center, place your words so that they "move" through the thirds of the page, over a background that is subtle enough to not compete with the words.

HAVE NO FEAR!

It's OK if your words or images "fall off" the page! Whether purposely or accidentally, having only half a stamped letter, or part of an image, at the edge of your page can suggest repetition, continuous movement, or fragmented or harried feelings.

While straight lines and separations imply stability, diagonals and curves imply movement. Try arranging elements on the page so they separate the page diagonally. You might place striped paper to cover a diagonal section on one third of the page, and then place floral paper to cover the remaining diagonally shaped two-thirds. Your words, or the image itself, will be straight, but the grouping or background creates a diagonal split on the page. You can also place images or text in a V-shape, to direct the eye to your focal point. As you look at our journal page samples that follow, notice that simple graphic or color elements make a big difference in the "artistic" appeal of the page.

memory tripping altered book

MEMORY TRIPS

A GOOD HIDING-PLACE

SIMPLE SUPPLIES

old book, trimmed to a point at the top • glue stick • gesso • paintbrush • acrylic paint • acrylic glazing medium • paper towel • cosmetic sponge • red inkpad • Magic Mesh • gel medium • photo • brayer • rubber stamps • black inkpad • decorative paper • stencil • clear label or sticker paper

Let's have some fun with composition as we take a trip down memory lane. Our house-shaped Memory Tripping journals literally house bits of our past; they help us remember who we used to be, and let us visit people who have passed away or moved away. In these journals, Poppa Dave is still fishing with our brothers, and we all do still live on the same street.

1 Begin with a book cut to a point at the top so it is house-shaped. If you cannot find one at a craft store, cut the corners off an old book with a craft saw. To make the pages sturdy, glue every other page together with glue stick. Cover the first spread of pages with gesso and let dry.

Mix equal parts glazing medium and acrylic paint. Using a paintbrush, cover one page with the glaze mix. Blot the painted page with a paper towel to create texture. Repeat on the facing page.

2

Use a cosmetic sponge to stencil red ink onto the page, through a piece of mesh. This adds some texture onto the pages. Apply gel medium to the back of your photo and adhere it to the center of the left page. Burnish it down with a brayer.

Stamp a few stars in black ink randomly over the two pages. Stamp out your words using alphabet stamps and the red ink. Use the larger set for the right page and the smaller set for the left page.

Tear off little strips of the decorative paper and adhere them to the corners of the photo using a glue stick.

Apply gesso to the entire front cover and let dry. Mix equal parts acrylic paint and glazing medium. Paint the bottom, square portion. Paint the roof portion with a different color. When the roof is dry, stencil texture over it using a cosmetic sponge, a third paint color and a star stencil.

Computer-generate your title text, and print it out on a clear label or sticker paper. Adhere the door to the front of the house with gel medium, then apply your title.

Cherries in the Pink Room

Notice that the stamped cherries are in the center third of the page, and the bend in the stem "nudges" the eye to the right page. If the cherries had been stamped on TOP of the contrasting pinstripe, they would not have been seen as equal focal points and would have been too busy.—Linda

cherries in
the pink
room

Rainy Day

Down our long, green-carpeted hallway with the green textured wallpaper was the closet where Mom stored "rainy-day surprises!" The contrast of the textured green with the cloudy sky reminds us of childhood surprises. The tag in the center third makes the words prominent. The key words on the right page are in the bottom third.—Linda

from the
closet
that smells
funny

rainy day
surprises

HOW SISTERS living their dreams, WAIT

How Sisters Wait

We sure don't "wait" to dive into peanut butter and chocolate chips! This blue-glazed page creates a feeling of open time, while the words, arranged in an upside-down pyramid form, create movement and drama. I placed the larger words across the top third of the page, smaller words in a shorter line in the middle third, and a shorter word in the bottom third. I put the spoon of goodies right where horizontal and vertical lines cross. Waiting ain't so bad... —Linda

Congratulations! You are about to enjoy the World's Ultimate Chocolate Experience!

* A midnight snack
   * With ice cream
   * Shared with giggles
* A bad day made better
   * At every celebration, even the smallest

BARBARA'S CAKE

Barbara's Cake

One bite of Barbara's Ultimate Chocolate Experience will send you on a heavenly trip. Barbara's Cake gets center stage in the right two-thirds of the page, with my ode to its riches wafting like a chocolate aroma off to the left. This page is actually full of memories, each conjured by the words Barbara's Cake, so I wanted those words to stand out against the fudgy browns and steamy whites. The red Dymo labeling did the trick. —Linda

MOM'S ADVICE: NEVER LEAVE THE HOUSE without LIPSTICK ON

Mom's Advice

Mom's advice is as good now as it was in the 1950s, when it originated. The black, white and pink tones are nostalgic. The jagged words create movement, as does the angle of the photo. —Linda

On a Hot August Night

You can feel the flames jumping up here! Placed in the bottom third, the flames spotlight the words and still capture lots of attention. The words remind us of the Neil Diamond song, playing on the drive. They mimic the jiggle of a car ride and lead your eyes on a journey through each third of the page. And it's OK the stamped clock "falls off" the edge! Time was lost!—Linda

Daisies

You can see the thirds in this completed piece! Whenever I see daisies now, they remind me of the wild daisies blooming all around the beautiful garden where I got married. I alternated words and pictures in the thirds of this page, weaving in the colors of the garden. The green in the upper right corner highlights the word daisies, and suggests their stems.—Linda

GET GOING:
Conversations With Me

Some of the best conversations we've ever had occurred in our own minds! Our silent promises, curses and witticisms play loudly to our spirits, and can feature prominently in a journal all their own. As we are often told, "It's the thought that counts!" In these journal pages, your thoughts are finally counted and respected. Whether our inner conversation is lighthearted or about ripping out someone's heart, we've found that it is a lot easier to let a feeling pass if we recognize it, express it, and wave good-bye as we turn the page on it. Visual journals allow us to be creatively mindful and to release ourselves and others. So, more and more, instead of trying to escape anger, frustration or embarrassment, we turn them into colors, shapes and words we can journal!

Turning your internal dialogues into journal pages is like peeling back the proverbial onion skin. You will see more layers than you realized you had, and you might shed some tears. But the tears wind up making you laugh too. This is an easy place to practice composition, because your words usually will be the focal point, and you can choose minimal or symbolic images and colors.

To journal these conversations, you must first realize they are occurring. Listen to the words behind your heartbeats. Whisper to yourself as you lie in bed, unable to sleep. Rewind the tape running in your head and play it back, slowly. Smile when you imagine something really funny. Hum along with that song you can't shake, as you visualize its colors splashed on a page. As you go about your day, take notes of your inner conversations. Our inner dialogues run from silly fashion commentary to nearly maniacal proclamations. Sometimes they are rhetorical questions even we cannot answer. Get some good hot chocolate, a piece of Barbara's Cake (see pages 60 and 126) and a few basic journaling supplies, and have a nice long chat with someone fascinating: *YOU!*

Start TODAY
This is the beginning of something GREAT.
Travel. Art. Us. what

I'm Done

Several voices were screaming and shrieking in my head at once: "I'm going nuts!" "I am DONE" "NO MORE" "I'm cracking up!" You can hear the shouting from the almost offensive purple background. The page is "cracking up" primarily in the middle third, and the cracks do not compete with the lettering in the top third. The nut is placed off-balance, and touches where the thirds intersect. If I need to remember to say "no!" I look at this page.—Linda

Purple Hand

I don't really believe in conspiracies, unless they apply specifically to me. I swear, some days, people conspire to ignore me. But I am on to them, and I've journaled about it to prove it. I used my handwriting font and an image of my traced hand to symbolize me reaching out to communicate. The absence of color highlights the words, which could otherwise have been lost next to the long fingers. —Linda

Some days, I am not sure if I am whispering or if everyone around me is going deaf

63

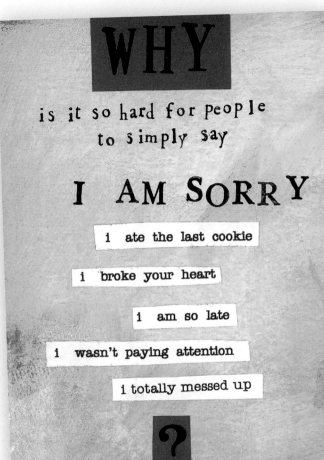

WHY

is it so hard for people
to simply say

I AM SORRY

i ate the last cookie

i broke your heart

i am so late

i wasn't paying attention

i totally messed up

?

I'm Sorry

This conversation floated through my head several times in one week. I painted on glazes, then rubbed some paint off, for an airy background. The black lettering really stands out and is the focal point. The text forms a backward S-shape on the page, creating movement and leading your eyes through the thirds. Though "I am sorry" is not on gray paper, the larger text gives it prominence.—Linda

Letting it Go

When I really want something, I imagine it's a kite, and I let it float into the sky; I let it go. I painted over gesso with light blue paint and quickly dabbed some off, to create an expansive sky. I painted white clouds traced in pencil, and stamped on the words. The kite is just a piece of a document I was working on. With the words in the bottom third, the kite flies free and unobstructed.—Linda

**LETTING
IT GO.**

I'm Invisible

The contrasting of red with black and white is dramatic—very visible. By placing my "invisible" face on the far right, I balanced the weight of the heavy colors and underscored the gap between who I wanted to be and who I felt I was. I did the lettering in handwriting with white paint, using a thin brush. The arrow points toward my eyes, because this is about seeing myself.—Linda

I AM Invisible. I want to BE Visible.

No Ideas

On a day when I felt empty, as if I had no ideas, I just wrote my feelings into my journal. The words are the visual element on these pages, rather than an image. I chose empty, block-letter text and filled the empty spaces with colors. Just as color brings life to my empty spaces, a bit of color makes these pages lively. When you have a lot to say, pick a font that mirrors your feeling, and go with it!—Linda

I HAVE NO IDEAS. NOTHING. ZILCH. ZIP. I AM AFRAID I WILL NEVER HAVE AN IDEA AGAIN. WHAT WILL HAPPEN TO ME?

WILL I HAVE TO THROW AWAY MY PAINTS AND PAPERS AND GET A REAL JOB? ONE WITH A DESK? THIS CAN'T BE HAPPENING TO ME RIGHT NOW, NO WAY.

FEAR BUSTER NO. 4

I CAN'T DRAW

We remember seeing a friend's so-called "sketch" book of her trip to France and thinking, "Doesn't sketch mean 'rough drawing'?" We dipped some more bread in the Nutella she brought us, gazed jealously at the portrait-perfect images of open markets and castle turrets, wiped the crumbs from our mouths, and asked her earnestly, "How do you have time for flea markets when you spend so much time drawing everything?"

We cannot draw as our friend does, but we don't let that little detail intimidate or hinder us. We have discovered, actually, that we can draw fairly well—when we have the inclination. So never limit yourself with old descriptions of your abilities! With our Personal Palettes handy, we don't even have to be able to draw a nose, a city skyline, or what *exhausted* looks like. Simply using the colors and patterns associated with a certain person, place or emotion will evoke the images we seek even better than our often frustrating attempts to draw a perfect picture. Remember, your visual journal pages are for you, so it does not matter if no one else understands the cues or hidden meaning in your art. Chances are, others will pick up on your message (if you care to share it with them) just as you probably see so much in our pages.

With imagery as with words, the secret is to simplify. Don't fret over drawing a closet full of rainy-day surprises. Instead, sit back, close your eyes, and see what shapes, colors and textures come to mind when you conjure up your fun childhood memory. Use those as your background colors and the accent elements for your words. If, for example, you want to journal about a day at the beach, don't pull your hair out trying to paint shimmering waves like acclaimed marine-life artist Wyland. Try this: Lightly paint a golden beigy color on the bottom third of your page. Above that, paint a third of the page blue. Finally, paint the top third a lighter blue, blending it into the darker blue below. What does it remind you of? The beach! Then, on top of your sand, sea and sky, place words or images where your Rule of Thirds grid lines intersect.

By using just three colors, you can "draw" many scenes. Experiment with acrylic paint, watercolors, crayons, sponged-on ink (so easy!) or torn papers glued on the page. Play around with different color combinations, and keep your creations to inspire journal pages later! Try this: Make the bottom third of the page green. Then color two-thirds light blue, blending into darker blue. There you have it—a welcoming summer field. Or springtime in Wales. Color a curving third of another page green, then leave a bit of white, paint the rest juicy red, and you've got watermelon-fresh summer. Sponge some gray, dark blue and purple on your page, and you are ready for a thunderstorm—or stormy emotions.

If you cannot draw the bucket you want on your "beach," or the umbrella for the downpour of your tears, or the perfect rose, cut one out from wrapping paper, a magazine or decorative paper, or use a rubber stamp. You can even draw just the basic, geometric shape of the object and color it in, and everyone will know what it is.

HAVE NO FEAR!

Don't stop yourself from using an image or color in your journal page just because you've used it in a previous page. Repetition is a part of life.

Pretend your journal pages are one big word-association game. Instead of being literal, think abstractly: What impressions *POP* in my head when I imagine that hotter-than-hell drive back from Vegas? *Fire!* When we think about escaping to Wales, we see *grass, flowers, sheep, plaid* . . . People, too, can inspire staccato-like images popping before your eyes. Our brother Tod: *smiles, peanut butter.* Brother Lee: *flashing, typewritten, courier-font, letters.*

Express your world and the characters in your life symbolically. Remember the mantra: *simplify.* Choose one primary symbol for the experience you are journaling (it may comprise a few parts—like the cut pieces of a picture) and two accents. Less really can be more. Remember, your background paints or paper are another accent. Don't fear you have to draw lots of detail. Choose to journal either about a detail or about the big picture; journal the process or the achievement; journal the cause or the effect. For example, you can show the broken teacup that was the last straw in making you nuts, or you can journal the feeling of having gone completely nuts.

If you can draw like a master, wonderful! If you can bring us Nutella from France, even better! If you do not feel like drawing, don't have the time to draw, or just think you can't, your visual journal pages will still look *magnifique!*

On Empty

Drained, used up, not a drop of me left. I felt "on empty." But how do you draw that feeling? You don't! I slathered the page in red paint and drybrushed black around the edges. I used a picture of an empty gas gauge to represent me, and printed my words from the computer, creating a black background for them. My imagery and colors made this a fast page that quickly helped me vent my feelings!—Karen

As the Sun Set on the City

When I see a city skyline, it looks like rectangles, triangles and squares all ganging up on each other. Interesting textures and patterns add life to these geometric shapes. I layered the shapes on the page, overlapping each other, as buildings do. The sun is setting in the upper right.—Linda

As the sun went down, we wandered through the city.

SOMETIMES
WE EAT
BREAKFAST
FOR DINNER

and

SOMETIMES
WE EAT DESSERT
FOR
BREAKFAST

Breakfast for Dinner

Rather than try to draw a table, I tore and glued on a piece of checkered decorative paper that immediately reminded me of a tablecloth. The fried egg is just a white circle with a yellow circle in the center. I stamped big letters, so they did not get lost in the breakfast rush. —Linda

Dessert for Breakfast

When you are in the mood to draw, you can always start with simple shapes. This pie slice is basically a combination of triangles and rectangles. Try it—you can draw pie easier than you can bake it! You'll want to set up a slice or two, to model, of course. —Linda

getting to know me
(self-portrait)

SIMPLE SUPPLIES

watercolor paper • acrylic paint in three colors (We used ivory, blue and magenta—choose what you like.) • glazing medium • flat brush • gel medium • decorative paper (We used sheet music. Choose paper that represents a favorite song, a treasured memory or a wish, perhaps.) • brayer • paper towel • photo (We used a flower, the "self" in this portrait. Select something to be "you.") • accent item (We used a strip of film negative; you can use something representing a hobby, skill or talent.) • text of your choice

Now it's time to look in the proverbial mirror: How will *YOU* symbolize you? Our bodies are the amazing vehicles we use for travel and movement here on Earth, yet we are not our bodies. What image conveys who you are, unlimited by your body? Consider what color embodies you and what shape represents you. You can make a remarkably revealing self-portrait without drawing a thing!

In trying to characterize yourself, you will find you have many roles. You can create a symbolic self-portrait of you at play, another for you in your family role, one for you independently. Show yourself as a parental figure, as a student figure, as a giver or a receiver, as a plant you relate to, or as an animal whose nature matches your own. Freely, artfully, express how you may be seen or the forms in which you may appear.

As varied as your self-images are, so too can the form vary. They can be doodled, painted, layered with collage papers, or created solely with words. You are creating *YOU*. Make it your way. What color is your soul? What shape is your spirit? Let us get to know you.

GETTING TO KNOW ME (SELF-PORTRAIT)

Paint your watercolor page a solid color, using acrylic paint mixed with an equal amount of glazing medium. Choose a color that represents a part of you (I used magenta, because this portrait is the "me" in my garden, and these colors suit me there). Let your brushstrokes show. Adhere your chosen decorative paper with gel medium to the right side of the page. Burnish the paper well with the brayer.

Choose your other two colors to blend on the decorative paper. I mixed some ivory paint with a bit of glazing medium and drybrushed it over the decorative paper, then let it dry. I then mixed one part blue paint to three parts glazing medium. I brushed the mixture over the right side of the decorative paper, and rubbed off some of the paint with a paper towel. Create a texture that feels right for you. The dry brush gave a garden-weathered look, which seemed right for me.

Mix equal parts of your main color (for me, magenta) and glazing medium, and roughly paint a square just above the center of the page. This will act as a shadow for your personal collage element. Rub off excess paint with a paper towel.

Use the same two colors to make an accent on your page. For example, add, but do not mix, a bit of ivory to the remaining blue paint, and load the brush with both colors. Drag the brush in vertical strokes down the bottom left half of the page.

Using gel medium, adhere your photo and accent item(s) to the page. "You" look GREAT!

home is where the art is (journal box)

opening up

SIMPLE SUPPLIES

wooden box • gesso • flat brush • acrylic
paint • gel medium • images for the lid •
cosmetic sponge • red inkpad • two sizes of
stencils • black inkpad • alphabet stamps

Something about opening a box and peeking in it is magical. (Unless of course, you're Pandora—in which case, we would recommend keeping the lid closed!) Discovering art inside, pages and pages of it, in different shapes, sizes and colors, is a real treasure. When guests come to our homes, they love looking in our journal boxes and discovering tidbits about us that they may find surprising. The funny thing is, we love looking in each other's journal boxes, even the ones we have looked in hundreds of times before!

Your journal box is a home for loose journal pages, and you personalize it by journaling right on the box. You can keep all your loose pages in one box, or have some boxes for certain types of loose journal pages. Linda has a journal box for "Self-Portrait" and "I Am" pages. The top of the box says, "Me, a Name I Call Myself." Karen has a journal box for "Buttons" pages, and her kids add their Buttons, too. Choose two or three colors for your box, a photo if you wish, and some words that suit the type of pages your box will house. Don't be surprised if you yourself often delight in the treasures inside!

73

HOME IS WHERE THE ART IS (JOURNAL BOX)

1

Cover the outside of the box with gesso; let dry. Paint the entire box with your chosen color of paint (we used yellow).

2 When the paint is dry, use gel medium to adhere your images to the lid of the box.

3

Ink up your sponge with red ink, and add color to the edges of the box. You may want to add more color in some areas than others.

4 Add texture with the same ink and sponge, using the smaller stencil. Then, do the same using the larger stencil.

5 Add a few touches of black ink to the box edges, using an inked sponge. Stamp your words in black ink, using the alphabet stamps.

I Explore

One of my personal symbols is a perfect pear. The pear shape is feminine and comforting. Combined with other elements, it can also be a bit silly. That's me! This page tells the story of my self-discovery.—*Linda*

I See it All

Along my journey of self-discovery, I realized another symbol for me is a chair. I like to invite people in, and I'm often more comfortable observing the party than being the party. The colors are warm and celebratory, yet still reserved.—*Linda*

Home

For some reason, people see me as a sturdy, reliable, safe and comforting shelter, so a home is a symbol for me. Sage green is my calming, soothing color, so I made the house green. Branches and trees stand for growth, taking chances and learning. On this page, I collaged the house and rubber-stamped the trees, over a painted background. The text is vinyl letters and words from a book.—*Linda*

Entry Denied

On those days when I wish no one would come to call, I am a brick wall. If they do come to call, all entry is denied. I need space of my own sometimes. This easy page (combining simple line-drawing, watercolor and rubber stamps) conveys a lot of strength because it is direct and unapologetic.—*Linda*

GET GOING:
Pieces of Me

Try gathering various images and textures that combine to create you, and make a personality quilt showing all the pieces of you. While your self-portrait zoomed in and magnified a part of you, combining the "pieces of you" for one journal entry expresses the big picture. You can even make this a really big picture, if you want. Do a spread across two journal pages, or one large page, or a scroll.

Because you will have several images or patterns on the page, a solid-color background is usually best, though not required. Choose the color or color wash from your Personal Palette that represents you to *you*, or a color that highlights your elements. You might include images that hint at milestones in your life, nicknames you've gone by, habits for which you are teased, places you love to be, people you cherish, patterns that speak to you, tastes you crave . . . the little bits of information we would need if we wanted a full picture of you. You'll be surprised how many pieces of you there are!

Start TODAY
This is the Beginning of
something GREAT.
Travel. Art. US. what

MY STORY

NEW

CAPTURING a moment.

Canterbury Cathedral
Photographic Permit
For Personal Use Only

£1

SHREWSBURY ABBEY

PERMIT FOR PHOTOGRAPHY AND VIDEOGRAPHY

For Private Non-Commercial Use Only

Please note that this permission does not allow the use of video recorders
during Worship and other events. Enquiries concerning photography and videography for
commercial purposes should be made to the Vicar (01743

Date of issue. 10 · 6 · 00

We explored China Town which was lively and colorful, even with a light rain. We made our way to
Union Square for dinner at a French Jazz cafe.

Thanksgiving '02

San Francisco

HOTEL CARLOS

ESPAÑA FUENTE

CONEY ISLAND
CINCINNATI, OHIO

GAMES

TEN POINTS

CONEY ISLAND
CINCINNATI, OHIO

CONEY ISLAND
AMERICA'S FINEST AMUSEMENT PARK
CINCINNATI, OHIO

GAMES

TEN POINTS

FEAR BUSTER NO. 5

I DON'T HAVE
ANY EPHEMERA,
AND I DON'T KNOW WHAT IT IS

It's funny that a ragtag mess of stuff could have such a scientific, if not romantic, pretentious name. Literally, *ephemera* means "a range of collectable items that were originally designed to be short-lived." Don't let it scare you. "I'm preserving ephemera!" is simply the declaration that gave dignity back to pack rats everywhere. What's more, you *do* have ephemera—trust us.

Ladies, look in your purse. You have receipts, lists, notes, coupons, buttons, wrappers, ribbon—a veritable garage sale worth of ephemera right there! Gentlemen, that top desk drawer is a fine place to begin: cards, notes, wrappers, golf tees, foreign coins, receipts, ticket stubs. We all have photographs, and we all have brains, which photograph the sights, sounds, tastes, touches and smells of our lives. That's "ephemera." The funny thing about ephemera is it means something of no lasting significance; yet, these tidbits from our lives carry great significance.

Life and time are fleeting, and by keeping ephemera and using it in journals, we capture the fleeting. How quickly we otherwise forget the things we thought we could never forget—our miracles and our miseries, both; and perhaps if we could remember them, we might see the secret to our miracles, and the miracles within our miseries. One thing is for certain: We would laugh a lot more, even at the things that once made us cry.

As a start, try this: Keep notes and drawings about your day on napkins, tags and torn bits of paper while you sit in the car waiting to pick up the kids (or at the drive-through window at Krispy Kreme . . . *not* while the car is moving) and add them later to your journals or albums. Keep fortunes from fortune cookies; grab Metro maps from your sister while she is trying to plan your itinerary; keep ticket stubs from plays and movies; take decorated paper coasters from cool restaurants; pick up free newspapers from towns you visit; when your kids unwrap presents, snatch neat ribbons; keep wrappers from your favorite candies, especially in foreign countries. Soon, you'll have a box full of ephemera!

The obvious things to keep from trips to new places are maps, ticket stubs, stamps, e-mails you sent and received, newspapers, train schedules, printed shopping bags, and hotel receipts. Collect the same things in your hometown. Gather things that remind you of your daily events. A receipt for a prescription, a flyer advertising a local play, phone messages and bits of e-mails are all great for use in your journal.

When you are relaxing at home (ha-ha!), cut out interesting and inspiring words or entire phrases from books and magazines, preferably after your housemates have finished reading them. Then, keep a little plastic bag of words handy to use in your journal pages. Fill the bag with words in different fonts, colors and moods. Simply picking a word or phrase from the bag will prompt your journaling, or you can arrange your clippings by subject so you can find just the right accent when you need it.

Photographs from your past and present, even "bad" photos that cannot go in your albums or scrapbooks, are perfect ephemera for journals. Just paint or write over the blurry parts of the photos, or over the people you don't like. When you are at yard sales, pick up old postcards, letters, photos, magazines and books for ephemera. Pick them up off the street, for that matter. Once you start looking, you will find lots of free ephemera, which other people might foolishly call junk, all over town. Bear in mind, it is generally considered bad form to take ephemera directly from the hands or purse of someone else.

GET GOING:
Altered Travel Journal

You ask, "I can't remember where I went this morning—how will I remember what ephemera goes with which city once I get back from a trip? I haven't even unpacked from my vacation two years ago. How on earth will I ever find time to journal while everything is still fresh in my mind?"

There is no time like the present, and no present like time, we say! Use your time on vacation to journal, as part of your gift to yourself. Journal right in the travel guide you brought with you, and you will remember not only where you hiked and ate, but how you found those dream spots. You can rub your pages against the ground to grab the color of the earth, and dry flowers between the pages to bring the fields home with you. Use a highlighter to mark the key parts of the guide, and comically revise the text as needed.

Tote a glue stick and small scissors with you, and you can add mementos from restaurants, theaters, gardens and train stations while you are there. Write your impressions in the margins of the travel guide, add some fibers or ribbon if you like, and a perfect memory is completed.

Start TODAY
This is the beginning of something GREAT.
Travel. Art. Us. what

San Francisco

I kept menus and flyers passed out on the streets of San Francisco and added them to our travel guidebook. I used a glue stick to glue them to the guidebook page in layers. On the left is a street map of the area where our hotel and the restaurants were. I like the contrast of the red next to the many colors on the right page, and the red reminds me of Chinatown.—Linda

Conservatory

We spent a perfect afternoon at the Conservatory of Flowers. To remember it, I stapled the ticket into the guidebook, and painted inside a few of the colors that were so prominent. I added some of my pictures from the day and bits of the Conservatory brochure, with handwritten details about the trip.—Linda

GET GOING:
Collections Journal

Displaying collectibles on your nightstand, buffet and coffee table is so twentieth century, so common. Collecting unusual bits of your life and making artful journals from them—now, that is mod and fascinating! A collections journal can house actual things you collect, or pictures of the thing, or words about that collectible. Horses, for example, could not actually be in the collections journal, but you could make wild, adventurous journal pages showcasing a collection of horse memorabilia, horse-riding experiences and poetry about horses. You could even cut a plastic horse in half lengthwise, and attach it to the cover.

In your collections journal, you can have fun experimenting with different ways to display and represent things you collect in your life. You can also examine parts of your life as a collection, which you may not before have seen that way. Linda collects ephemera from her outings with three of her good friends, finding new ways to journal about their shared shopping, giggling and art experiences. Karen is a lipstick-a-holic and has a journal dedicated to her lipstick obsession, with doodles, lipstick marks, antique advertisements and favorite brand and color names. We both collect fortune cookies, and love creating pages filled with good fortune. When we are done with a phase, obsession or collection, the journal pages serve as vivid reminders of where we have been and where we are headed!

Start TODAY
This is the beginning of something GREAT.
Travel. Art. Us. what

Shopping Spree

Receipts are more than garbage, tax deduction backups and purse lining! I saved the receipts from some laughter-filled afternoons with friends and used them as the backdrop for this spread. I enhanced it with Dymo labeling, cutout words and rubber-stamping.—*Linda*

First Entertainment Credit Union
P. O. Box 100 • Hollywood, CA 90078-0100

THE EXPERIENCE.

Thank you for banking
with Washington Mutual.

Transaction Summary

$$$

SHOPPING WITH
MARLENE AND JUDY

SPREE.

CHICO'S

Capturing a Moment

At some tourist attractions, you must purchase a photo permit before snapping away for your travel journal. I captured the moment of paying to capture a moment by gluing my photo fee ticket into my collections journal. I added rubber-stamping and cutout words, and stuck on a local postage stamp to balance the lettering on the left.—*Linda*

CAPTURING ✳

a moment.

✳

Canterbury Cathedral
Photographic Permit
For Personal Use Only

SHREWSBURY ABBEY

PERMIT FOR PHOTOGRAPHY AND VIDEOGRAPHY

For Private Non-Commercial Use Only

Please note that this permission does not allow the use of
during Worship and other events. Enquiries concerning
commercial purposes should be made to the Vicar (01743

Date of issue: 10·6·00

We explored China Town which was lively and colorful, even with a light rain. We made our way to
Union Square for dinner at a French Jazz cafe.

Thanksgiving '02

San Francisco

China Town

*I LOVE the beautiful Chinese papers I get during
our annual Thanksgiving trips to San Francisco.
I used a piece as my background here, and layered
it with a photo of my shoes (we walked all over
the city) and computer-generated text printed on
clear sticker sheets.—Linda*

LEARN CHINESE - Good
Hao

the quality of the day
small achievement.
Numbers 6, 9, 18, 23, 25, 34

You are a lover of words,
someday you will write a book.
Lucky Numbers 8, 11, 24, 25, 34, 38

true!

Advancement will come
with hard work.
Lucky Numbers 6, 13, 19, 33, 34, 43

You have a reputation for being
straightforward and honest.
Lucky Numbers 2, 7, 10, 31, 33, 38

Reasonable people endure;
passionate people live.

Fortunes

*We both collect fortunes from the fortune cookies
at our favorite Mongolian restaurant, and
from the best fortune cookie baker ever, in San
Francisco. Just as our "fortune" can change course
from moment to moment, the fortunes move
across and down this page, almost dancing.
I painted my page with colors of prosperity
and luck, glued on some favorite fortunes, and
highlighted the center to draw attention and
add focus to this page.—Linda*

my day unfolds journal

SIMPLE SUPPLIES

watercolor paper • scissors • pencil • ruler • stylus (or bone folder) • computer-generated text (mine is on mulberry paper) • glue stick • black inkpad • cosmetic sponge • decorative paper scraps • found images • rectangular piece of decorative paper (for cover decoration) • white paper • decorative paper shipping tag • keyhole rubber stamp • decorative fibers • ribbon

A Day in the Life of You. How does your typical day unfold, from rise to rest? The common events that move your days along appear like snapshots in this accordion journal. This is a journal you can make anew from time to time, to see how a typical day for you has changed.

We like lighthearted images, easily created with a bit of texture and a photo or drawing. Simple graphics, with bold colors and big sizes, quickly convey what's happening during the day and give the journal a modern, pop-art feel. Alternating the placement of your words on each panel of the accordion, creates a feeling of movement. With a series of "My Day Unfolds" journals, you can tell the stories of your life at different jobs, both before and after having children, with good bangs and bad bangs, and at home or abroad.

Brutal honesty makes the journals funny and genuine. In one of her accordion journals, for example, Karen professes her workday begins by fighting frizz and ends by searching for her car. Linda's journal confirms suspicions about how much time she spends reading e-mails. If you mistakenly thought nothing ever happens in your life, have fun trying to pare your day down to six panels!

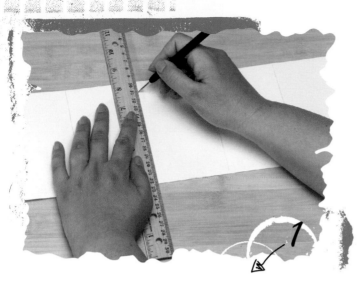

1

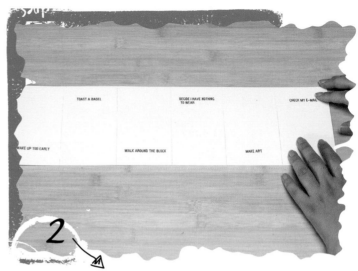

2

Trim a piece of watercolor paper to 5" × 18" (13cm × 46cm). With the paper sitting horizontally, starting from the left side, make a light pencil mark on the paper every 3" (8cm). Score a vertical line at each mark, using a ruler and a stylus.

Erase all the pencil lines. Cut out all your computer-generated text (random shapes are fine). Glue your text into the panels of your journal booklet. Alternate where you glue the text: Place the text at the bottom of the first panel, then the top of the second panel, and so on.

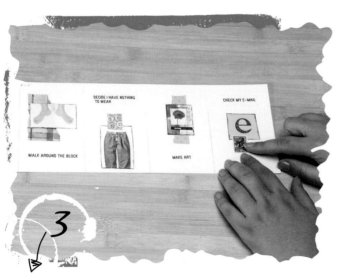

3

4

Using the black inkpad and the sponge, add a bit of black ink to the edges of all your images. Tear decorative paper to "frame" each image. Glue each piece of decorative paper and each image in its corresponding panel. Create accordion folds along the score lines.

Ink the edges of the rectangular piece of decorative paper, then glue it to the front of the journal. Print "My Day Unfolds" on white paper, cut out, then glue to the decorative paper tag. Stamp a keyhole on the tag, below the title. Tie decorative fibers on the tag, and glue the tag layered on top of the rectangular paper on the front of the journal. Tie the whole journal closed with ribbon.

e v e r y day

I Wear This

I am famous for wearing the red scarf my mom knit for me. I think I have it on in every picture of me from 2004 to 2005. This page was simple: I drew the outline of the scarf in pen, filled it in with watercolor red, then stamped on the words. I almost started over when the words "every day" got stamped weird; then I remembered—it's OK if the stamps go weird!—Linda

Menu

Routine

My husband hates cilantro and I love it. He insisted that our wedding vows include my promise never to include cilantro in any meal I serve. Nevertheless, every night as I present a gourmet masterpiece before him, he asks, "Is there cilantro in this?" Note that I let my thoughts literally run off the page here, mimicking the way this routine goes on and on. I used a color copy of real cilantro as well.—Linda

—R O U T I N E—

"Is there cilantro in this?" he asks before eating anything. As if after ten years I still

Wake Up

Setting two alarms "just in case" is a silly routine from school days that I just cannot give up! I used a pre-painted red background (red = urgent!) and stamped on my words and the black sunbursts. I used a royalty-free clip art image of a clock, and printed it in negative and positive for morning and night. —Linda

WAKE UP

I always set two~
just in case one doesn't work.

my UNIFORM

black shorts that look like a skirt

V-neck T-shirt

Jacket

← RED shoes

Lipstick

Coach bag

My Uniform

Find what works and stick with it. In keeping with that saying, I wear the same thing every day (or so it seems). I wanted red to be dominant on this page, as in my wardrobe, so I used a light, complementary wash on the background. I stamped on the title and wrote in the details. —Linda

GET GOING:

"That Made My Day" Journal

Wake up and look for reasons to smile! Sprinkled throughout our days are little lifesaving events that deserve recognition. If you don't look for them, you might otherwise miss them; by planning to journal about what made your day today, you instead will have to choose between unexpected treasures you discovered, now that you are hunting.

Give thanks on the pages of your journal for the small gifts life gives you. (Thank *us*, on the other hand, with Barbara's Cake!) Remember that time you hadn't had a date in seven months and you screamed out loud, "All I want is for one man to call!" and then the phone actually rang and it was a real man, a man you wanted to talk to? Or that day you got the parking place right in front, and thank goodness, because it was raining when you came out, and you had no umbrella? What about the morning your back hurt so bad you could not get out of bed, even though your Chico's 50-percent-off coupon was expiring that day, and then the chiropractor fixed it all with one good twist?

Making someone else's day will make yours, too. Journal about the joys you receive and the joys you give. Ask yourself, "Am I looking to be happy?" Then make your day smile.

Start TODAY
This is the beginning of something GREAT.
Travel. Art. Us. what

Warm Breeze

In the midst of errands and responsibilities we'd love to shirk, a perfect leaf floating by, carried by a warm breeze, can make our day. I painted the background to match the heat of the day and the swirling breezes. I glued on a picture of a pretty flower I passed but could not take the time to smell, affixed flying leaves and colorful texture, then applied rub-on lettering. —Linda

Hug and a Promise Kept

Acceptance and love, trust and loyalty: Now, there are a few things that will make your day! The words were my focus here, so I stamped them over a lightly painted, joyful background. I used the hot pink dots to create movement and flow between the pages and to connect them. —Linda

Flowers at My Door

Since we were far younger lasses, we've been known for the retort "Say it with flowers!" Luckily, I married a man who does! The surprise of flowers at my door, for no reason at all, made my day. Using BIG rubber stamps is easy, and complements the primitive look of simple, hand-sketched flowers. For the flowers, I doodled with black pen, then colored them in with watercolor paint.—Linda

Lunch by the ocean with Marlene and Trudi on the day Judy "ditched" us.

Lunch by the Ocean

We had a wonderful girls' lunch by the ocean; the only problem was one of the girls didn't show. We laughed about her absence. The colors of the sea, sand and my friends are combined on this page, even though I did not actually draw any of those things. I chose decorative paper to represent each person and the water. Handwritten text suited the style of this entry best.—Linda

Adjust

Relief at last! The chiropractor adjusted my aching back and my outlook. I painted the background, then blended in images of a spine and vintage advertisements, both printed on clear sticker paper so the background would show through (almost like an X-ray). I painted the red circle and hand-stamped the word "adjust" so the letters were compressed and badly spaced—like my vertebrae.—Linda

IT IS EASY for a well person to be happy.

ADJUST

GET GOING:
Moments Journal

We've journaled about the large-scale routines, daily practices and random happy acts that compose our lives. Now, let's get out a magnifying glass and look close-up at a single moment. Try to focus on a breath. (Can you hear yourself blink? Linda can!) When you are stopped in your tracks, entranced by an inner or outer vision, remember that moment. What captured you? Was it the hummingbird perfectly poised at your lilies? The sound of your oldest friend's laughter on your answering machine? The heart-wrenching fear that you might have forgotten her birthday?

Get back into that moment: Paint its colors, attach its texture, write your fears. Reach back in your mind for past moments, too. Re-feel the moment when you opened an acceptance letter, saw all those presents under the tree, or tasted the best biscuits ever baked. Laugh through your journal page at the moment you realized you had glued the scarf on your neck to a collage. Your experience of your days will change as you remain aware of interesting moments to journal.

Start TODAY
This is the beginning of something GREAT.
Travel. Art. US. what

Mandy

We love our captured moments of our beloved Great Pyrenees, Mandy. She herded us through many days, spreading love and cheer to all who got to pet her adorable (though usually drooling) face. I painted this background in happy Mandy colors, and adhered her cute picture with masking tape. I added text from a book, with the words we now sadly say, "Where is she?"—Linda

Where is she?

Thai 'N I and Blink

Thai 'N I is a favorite family spot for Thai food, really nice servers and good fortunes! We spend many tasty moments there, asking deep questions of the fortune cookies. Both these pages are base-painted in red and black. The page on the left was collaged with an envelope decorated with pieces of a favorite menu. Inside the envelope is a tag punched from grass paper and collaged with a fortune.

In a contemplative moment, no doubt inspired by a fortune, I actually heard myself blink. (Karen says she has heard me blink for years, but I never believed her!) The right page is a black-and-white photocopy of my (nonblinking) face, collaged with green paper and Dymo labeling. Yes, I used Blopens around the edges!—Linda

Thai'N I

In
(b.   best barbeque
Blv.   shops. At Thai'N I Barbeque
       barbeque area is enclosed in glass but the
succulent Thai style ribs and chickens on the gril
              steady stream of customers.

I HEARD

MYSELF

BLINK

We Share

Sharing chocolate between friends; now, that's a moment to remember! Memorable because it IS unlike us to share a little candy bar. I took a bite out of a yummy bar and then photographed it for this page. I combined my original image with printed decorative "chocolate" paper and stamped words. The tag is punched decorative paper with magazine words cut out and embroidery floss for the string.—Linda

I'D HAVE TO DO IT ALL ALONE

If you laugh over your own journal page and no one hears it, is it still funny? Yes! Some may momentarily fear that they cannot be journaling while hanging out with their friends. Others may feel that without a group of friends to journal with, they will miss the fun of a shared experience, or lack inspiration for ideas, or feel inadequate without constant encouragement. First, you absolutely can journal with friends, both near and far. Second, your every moment sparks inspiration, we've given you all sorts of encouragement, and innumerable ways exist to share this artful experience. Remember too: As long as you have the Internet, you are never alone. As long as you have this book, you are never alone!

We challenge you to keep the art of journaling from your friends. It really cannot be done. Anyone who sees your journal books or your tempting journal box will immediately want to do it or revel in it! If you like to share your art journaling, your friends and family will love participating in it with you. Shhhhh! Even our husbands have journaled!

One of the gifts of journaling is the shared experiences your journal pages create. If you choose to open your journal pages to friends and family, everyone will be eager to discuss the many memories, wishes and images captured within—especially if you serve brownies! Comparing your different memories of the same event is great fun, and enables you to see the past from many perspectives. Howls of laughter, and deeper bonds, always accompany the opening of our "Buttons" journals with our friends. Now, we all laugh, or groan, in anticipation when we know one of our friend's buttons is about to be "pushed." You will always have one friend or family member dying to know if he has been memorialized in your journal pages. If you took our tip and used a symbol for this lovably annoying pal, he will never know just how many times he appears!

Your friends and family can actually join in the fun quite easily. You can involve them by incorporating their writing, their drawings, their memories or their comments into your journal pages. For example, when we go on a trip with family or friends, we bring one journal, and each night one of us writes in it on behalf of all of us. The scribe for the evening listens to the cacophony of comments, ideas and requests from everyone and creates a journal entry. She can include ticket stubs, menus, maps, receipts for mosquito-bite cream, stains from whatever she is eating at the moment, etc. The next morning, we all pass the journal around over breakfast, eager to read how the prior day was captured. There's no reason you can't do this at home; keeping a family journal or a friendship journal is easy and rewarding.

Others can journal with you on a daily basis, or at arranged journaling get-togethers, or on an impromptu basis. Catch 'em off guard—then they can't pretend they had a dentist appointment that day and not show up. Linda likes to surprise lunch guests with journaling projects. She introduces the projects before dessert, so no one in their right mind leaves! Everyone is thrilled with the result and asks for copies of their pages to use as note cards or to put in their own journals. Encourage your friends by telling them that even simple notes and doodles are meaningful to you and will make your journal special. Exclaim to them, in a supportive manner: "Have no fear! *YOU ARE ART!*" There are no bad journal pages, just empty ones, waiting for your unique imprint.

HAVE NO FEAR!

If your guest journalers still think they are "just not artistic," give them some friendly and easy composition tips. For a dynamic and energetic feeling, you can suggest arranging words or images on the paper so they follow an S- or a backward S-shape. This shape draws the eye over the page and keeps balance by forcing you to distribute words or images into each third, while avoiding a center focus.

GET GOING:
"My Life" Guest Book

We put out guest books for milestone events in our lives. This guest book is for the milestone people in our lives. For those you welcome not just to a reception or service, but for those who are invited to share your life. Linda keeps her guest book in her studio, and when friends come by, they "sign in." Her guest book pages are filled with much more than signatures: Linda varies the art supplies she keeps next to the book, so her guests can have fun experimenting for a few minutes each visit with different art media. Some weeks, the guest book table has paints, sometimes markers, sometimes old magazines and scissors. A basket of photos and decorative paper scraps is always nearby, because Linda just never cleans that up. Linda offers writing prompts for her guests on some pages too. Of course, some people have created many entries and love to look back at their years-old ones!

For the book itself, Linda uses an inexpensive (we're serious—99 cents) composition book, covered just as we showed you for the Buttons journal cover. You can use any kind of journal you want. Karen has had guests fill out 4" × 6" (10cm × 15cm) cards, which she later put in a photo album with pocket sleeves. We've also sent friends "interviews" through the mail, with self-addressed, stamped envelopes, so they can still be in the guest book, even from afar. So set out your guest book and get your par-tay started!

leave

A TRUE OFFERING
A COMMENT
A QUESTION
A MEMORY OF US
WORDS
COLORS
SHAPES
A SECRET PASSAGE
or a song

Intro Page (by Linda)

The many guests in my life are greeted with my special guest book—whether they like it or not! This friendly instructions page gives them gentle prompts for inspiration, and even the shy guests have made wonderful pages in my books. Your instructions page can include any prompts or ideas you want, or none at all. I wanted to make the book welcoming, so I used a yellow background and inked the edges of the paper to make it stand out. I stamped on words in various sizes and glued in the square-punched flower image. Small images are stamped in the background using shadow ink.

Loon Lake Collage (by Lee)

Our brother Lee created a collage by collecting images and expressions of our summers spent on Loon Lake in Washington. He stamped on the phrase constantly blasting across the lake from the snack bar: "Treat yourself and treat the kiddies." This page is a memory treat!

Hands (by Dustin)

Even Linda's husband, Dustin, snuck a page in here. He base-painted the page in reds and yellows, combined stamped text with handwriting, and cut out images along with a collection of personal photos. If Linda got her husband to journal, you can get your significant other to join in the art fun, too.

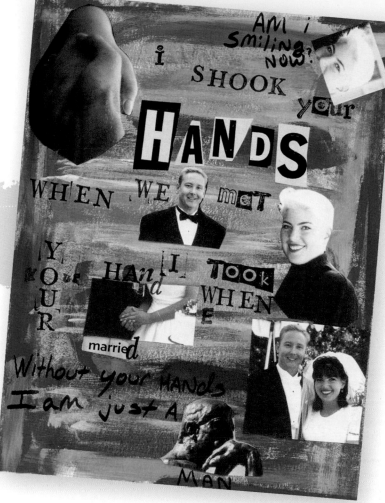

AM i smiling now?

i SHOOK your

HANDS

WHEN WE met

YOUR HAN I TOOk
YOUR WHEN
married E

Without your HANds
I am just A

MAN

split evenly, with me

When we visit there is color everywhere.
Even now, we talk about all
the important things in life.
The color of your spirit and friendship
has always been the same.
I can count on you for
anything, any time, any day.

I treasure our friendship!

-SUJ-

Heart (by Sujata)

When we were kids at school (and now), Sujata and Linda shared candies and life wisdom. Sujata's words are accented by a painted beige background with inked edges and collaged with a photo. Her text was computer-generated, then printed and glued in.

GET GOING:

Journaling Together

By keeping a journal with a friend, you get to know the dynamics of your friendship, yourself and your shared experiences better. There are many ways to work in a shared journal. You can have one journal shared between you, and you alternate possession. So, one week, you can have the journal and fill it with your insights, experiences, dreams, upsets and joys, and the next week, your friend can explore your entries and create her own. Another way is to choose a topic for your shared journal: Take turns journaling on that topic with one or many friends as you pass the book around.

You could also have a unifying theme for your journal, but change topics for the entries. For example, your journal theme could be "Roads Traveled," and your specific topic for one week might be "Memory Tripping." Another week's topic could be "Heavenly Hotels." A whole journal could be dedicated to your friendship or relationship.

You can also each keep a journal, and mail them back and forth, or meet for monthly journal exchange lunches. The benefit of having two journals going at once is that you each get to keep a finished journal. If you choose to keep one journal between you, you can always make a color copy of your page and glue that into the journal book, keeping your original. You also can copy your friend's page to keep. What we sisters like to do is trade off on who gets ownership of the journals. One of us will keep a journal at our house for a year or so, then the other gets it. Our friends (and we!) love to look at them again and again.

Start TODAY
This is the beginning of something GREAT.
Travel. Art. Us. what

Journaling With Friends
(by Linda, Judy & Marlene)

Linda and her friends Judy Claxton and Marlene Hazlewood spent an afternoon journaling fun days they have shared. They each journaled their perspective of one comical event, when Linda unexpectedly bumped into Marlene at a 50-percent-off rubber-stamp sale, and Marlene was actually on the phone to Judy, taking her stamp order as she shopped. Linda's page is base-painted blue and collaged with images and text. Judy's page is hand-drawn with handwritten text. Marlene's page is painted and collaged with cutouts.

Sleep

These pages are from our shared "Sisters" journal. One sister starts the page and the other finishes it. The theme of this journal is how we are alike or different, or: Why does Karen have bags under her eyes she could pack and take to Europe, and Linda looks so refreshed and cute? The base of these blue and white pages is an old page from a book that was coated with gesso, then painted. The text is stamped, Dymo labeled, and handwritten, with images that are rubber-stamped.—Linda & Karen

KAREN GOES TO BED EARLY

LINDA STAYS UP LATE

and we both dream about the same things

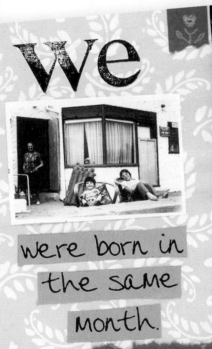

we were born in the same month.

DRAGON

1940,1952,1964,1976,1988,2000

You are eccentric and your life complex. You have a very passionate nature and abundant health. Marry a Monkey or Rat late in life. Avoid the Dog.

The Rooster

1945,1957,1969,1981,1993,2005

A pioneer in spirit, you are devoted to work and quest after knowledge. You are selfish and eccentric. Rabbits are trouble. Snakes and Oxen are fine.

1969

Born the Same Month

Yes, March is a good month for Barbara's Cake, Cinnabon certificates and Coach purchases! We covered these journal pages with decorative paper as our base and added rubber-stamped and computer-generated text. The rooster and dragon images are ephemera from our favorite Mongolian restaurant. We tore the images out and inked the edges with black ink for some definition.—Linda & Karen

Mother–Daughter Pages

Emily and I keep journals together of special days we have shared, embarrassing moments we have laughed over, recipes we baked (and wore!) and things that really push our buttons. As she graduates elementary school this year, we have some bittersweet pages, happy about her bright future and lovely present, and missing that cute little girl she used to be.

When journaling with kids, always remember that process is more important than outcome. I let Emily express herself her way. The pages really do capture her essence at a given age. Another thing to remember: Cover the floor with a cloth!—*Karen & Emily*

YUM

We wore more than we made!

O'Henry Cookies. These are fun to make and taste super yummy.

GET GOING:

Journaling Across the Miles

A blank envelope or postcard is the perfect canvas for a journal page! Both the postage stamp and the hand-canceling from foreign locations become intriguing parts of the journal page. The natural wear and tear (often literal) that happens to real mail adds character and charm to journaling, and ultimately creates an unexpected final piece of art. Your faraway friend won't know what her journal page will finally look like until you receive it! Of course, more journal material can be inside the envelope, but never overlook the envelope itself.

Incorporate the envelope into a journal page, and you have instantly symbolized your friend on the page. The delivery of mail from your friend also can be a "Moment" for your journal; it certainly can "Make My Day." Creating journaled mail art for your friends is another way to share your life with them, even when it seems you cannot because of the miles between you. You can pick a topic that you will mail each other journal pages about: brag about your amazing sales purchases, exchange top ten lists, pass the gossip on common friends. Even the mundane is interesting when journaled!

Emmy Mail

E-mail is mail art, too! Emmy's words of encouragement from far, far away inspired me and carried a lot of emotion. Adding pieces of her e-mail to my journals feels like I am putting Emmy right there on the page. I tore part of her e-mail to me and glued it into my journal, after brushing on paint as bright as her personality. I added a rubber-stamped image and glued on the first-class mail sticker.—Linda

FIRST CLASS MAIL ENCLOSED

linda- I REALLY think you are a monk (in training *grin*-does that make you a monk-ee??)....cause you give freely to us all the time with a smile and encouragement. Being attached to your art is a good thing because it's PART OF YOU-that's what we love.

emmy

FIRST CLASS POSTAL

MAIL

FROM FAR AWAY

Air Mail

Our friend Phil lives in England, but we e-mail and visit each other's families as often as possible, and immediately share new candies! The candy wrappers as well as the e-mail excerpts are great for shared journal pages and entries celebrating our friendship. For this page, I painted a blue background and glued on a photocopy of a favorite photograph of Phil. I stenciled dots around the perimeter of the picture and used adhesive and rub-on letters. Finally, I inked the edges.—Linda

Memories of home Spinning in my head... always make me dizzy

MAY 4 PM 850

PHOENIX MAY 4 PM 2005 85026

Ronda Kivett, Prescott Valley, AZ

Linda Woods
25852 McBean Pwy #104
Valencia, CA 91355

I can still smell my

mother's rose perfume...

Ronda's Mail Art

My friend Ronda sends gorgeous mail art envelopes, which I always fear the mail carrier will want to keep! Ronda Kivett's two envelopes here symbolize the seasons perfectly and share her life and observations with me before I even open the letter. —Linda

crossing and   curving toward the trestle,   on the far edge   of the   field

To: Linda Woods
25852 McBean Pwy #104
Valencia CA 91355

Spring is here... Vines are Climbing... birds are singing....

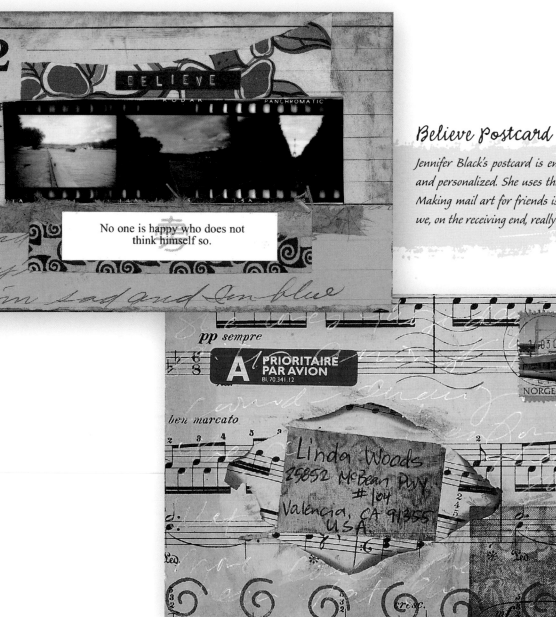

Believe Postcard

Jennifer Black's postcard is encouraging, philosophical and personalized. She uses the fortunes I always love. Making mail art for friends is fun and fulfilling, and we, on the receiving end, really appreciate it!

No one is happy who does not think himself so.

Music Envelope

This whimsical sheet music envelope from Erika Tysse is a journal in itself, enticing us to hop a train through Norway and sing about hills so alive with music, Austria is ashamed.

Red Mailbox

I love mailboxes in foreign countries, especially red ones! I created this envelope from graph paper (using an envelope template), then painted it bright yellow. I glued on a picture of a favorite mailbox from Italy and the typed address. I used rub-on lettering, which creates the feeling that the letters are bouncing off to the mailbox.—Linda

we put our memories in a red mail box

Le Poste a...... casa Tua
TELEFONA al **160** Servizio Opzionale vdi Asandelenco SIP
UFFICIO INFORMAZIONI POSTALI

Samantha Goldberg
19280 Cochise Court
The Creek, CA 9455

"And life is sweet."

Karen Dinino
2029 Ventura Blvd. # 47418
Woodland Hills, CA 91364

Flowerpot Mail Art

Cheery flowers are blooming on this postcard. I drew a basic flowerpot outline in pen. Then I used circle stencils to make the flowers and lightly brushed blue stripes on the pot. I added text from a book and printed out the address from my computer. I used green watercolor paint over the address to brighten it even more.—Linda

Umbrella

A real London Underground ticket is the template for this postcard. I enlarged the ticket on a copy machine, then glued it on the postcard. I stamped on the umbrella image and painted it pink. I chose a decorative postage stamp to complement the colors and theme of the postcard. The address is printed from my computer and glued on. —Linda

und ⊗ London Underground ⊗ London Underg

Rain, wind and freezing temps
Marks & Spencer
Boots
bad exchange rates
chocolate soup at harrods
umbrellas that don't work
laughing for hours
A keyboard with no squiggle mark

Brent Dinino
2029 Ventura Blvd. #47413
Woodland Hills, CA 91364

This side up • **Not** for resale
Issued subject to conditions - see over

This side up • **Not** for resale
Issued subject to conditions - se

"COME VISIT ME SO WE CAN SIT IN THE SWING BENEATH THE WEEPING WILLOW...

BUT, WE WON'T BE WEEPY. WE'LL BE LAUGHING!"

Weeping Willow

My friend Sujata loves this old picture of us, so I made a postcard by printing the picture in black-and-white and gluing it to a postcard. I also printed out on pink paper some words from our recent phone call—a moment we wanted to remember. The pink seemed nostalgic against the black-and-white, and stood out nicely. —Linda

FEAR BUSTER NO. 8

I CAN'T TAKE IT WITH ME

Contrary to what you might initially think, art journaling is an extremely versatile, portable hobby. For those journal pages that you wish to share with others, or when you want to share journaling itself with others, you can easily bring a pared-down journaling "essentials" kit and some spiral-bound index card books or pre-painted backgrounds to complete while on the go. We'll show you in this chapter ways you can take your journal with you around the house, around town or out of town.

Sometimes we journal while doing other things around the house; we call this multitasking. While Linda waits on hold for insurance representatives, she has colored markers and watercolor paper handy to journal about the frustrating experience. Karen brings Petal Point inkpads, shipping tags and a glue stick to the homework table: While she helps the kids do their work, she journals about something that made her day. In this way, we bring our journaling with us while we run errands and do household chores.

Because we so often think of things we want to journal, we keep a notebook for ideas in our car. Our journal pages often begin there. We admit to writing while driving, but it hasn't caused an accident yet. We can tear out the words we wrote and glue them on a journal page later, or redo those words in a computer font for the final page. If we didn't have this journal handy all the time, we would miss many journal-worthy moments throughout our days. We also let our passengers write in our notepads. It's so much fun to flip back through the notepad months later and see what a friend wrote while we were running into the drug store to grab a drink. Karen still has the first notepad she ever kept, in her first car ever, complete with notes from Linda at age twelve. She has another journal she took with her for hundreds of miles, and will take to her grave, probably!

When you go on vacation, you can bring no-mess inkpads, a glue stick, scissors, some cosmetic sponges and your pre-painted backgrounds and gather ephemera each day to create bright journal pages while you are there! We have made journal pages while on airplanes, using a pre-painted background, words cut from the airline magazine, and our trusty Uhu glue stick. This may make flight attendants nervous, and now due to airline regulations you must tear the words from the magazine (because your scissors will be confiscated at the security gate), but the pages make vivid memories. As we showed you on page 81, you can even journal right in your travel guide and not bother bringing another journal with you.

Not only can you journal while you walk about town, you can wear your journal while walking about town! Make some expressive Traveling Shoes (see page 121) to show where you've been or to imagine journeys to come. These shoes always invite comment and conversation—which leads to more journal pages! You can make shoes dedicated to favorite locations, or ones that capture your favorite walking tours, or just journal on shoes to carry your messages near and far.

HAVE NO FEAR!

Go ahead and write on that page. Just use your own handwriting, and journal with impact! If you do not like your handwriting, use someone else's handwriting! Select a handwriting font from your word processing program or download a free one from the Internet.

traveling shoes

SIMPLE SUPPLIES

white canvas shoes • water • acrylic paint
in several favorite colors • flat brush • scruffy
brush • fine-point permanent pen • stencil
• gel medium • chunky foam stamp • clear
acrylic spray sealer • ribbon (for laces)

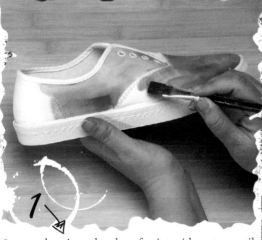

1 Separately mix each color of paint with water, until each reaches an inky consistency. Add solid blocks of color washes to your shoe, using the flat brush.

2 Paint simple objects on your shoe. We chose a landscape. We created a house with one stroke of color in a square, and the roof is just a triangle. The bushes are easy too—just little circles or small pounces with a scruffy brush. Remember, it's a SHOE; don't be too concerned with it being perfect. Loosely outline the shapes with a fine-point permanent ink pen. Create more drawings on the opposite side, if you like.

121

Using a fine-point pen, add journaling to the illustrated, side areas of the shoe. We wrote, "Wild Daisies."

Add texture to the toe panel, using a scruffy brush and a stencil. The stenciling can be random; you don't have to fill in the whole thing.

You can add collage elements with gel medium and a flat brush. The gel medium can be a little watered down. After affixing the elements to the shoe, once the area is dry, brush some additional gel medium over the top of the collaged portion.

A foam stamp can be used by applying paint directly to it with a brush, then stamping it onto the shoe. You can touch up areas with the paintbrush if you want.

HAVE NO FEAR!

If you want some of the panels to be like a landscape, just paint blue at the top and green along the bottom.

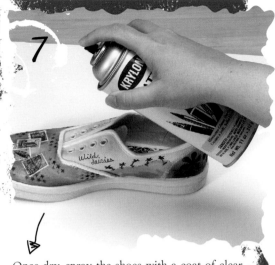

7

Once dry, spray the shoes with a coat of clear acrylic spray sealer.

8

Lace up your shoes with ribbon laces, and you are ready to take your journals on your travels!

HAVE NO FEAR!

Instead of ribbon, lace your shoes with fibers or fabric. If the ribbon gives you a tough time, just cut the ends to a point to make it lace easily. If you are a knitter, knit some I-cord laces! We'll hate you, but go ahead and make us jealous!

Shoes From Italy and England

These journaled shoes show scenes and ephemera from our trips to Italy and England. They were made following the same process as shown in the step-by-step photos; I just added some different types of ephemera or used different colors and stamping. Have fun with your traveling shoes, too!—Linda

GET GOING:
Traveling Journal Kit

Whether you are traveling to your kid's baseball game or to Burano, you can take journaling essentials with you to capture your impressions along the way. We know what you are thinking: "What's this going to cost me?" Have no fear! You can journal without spending a cent, if you need to, and we have. The most important thing you need to create an artsy journal takes up no space and is free . . . it is what is dancing in your head. Write your journal entries on whatever paper you have in your pocket, purse, glove compartment or carry-on. Use pen or pencil, and embellish your words with cutouts from magazines, free travel guides, paper napkins, local newspapers, maps, etc. Don't worry about using the "right" things; just use what you have. Your entry will be authentic and unique.

Essentials Kit

For an easy, small essentials kit to take with you from room to room in the house or to a hotel room on the go, we recommend the following:

glue stick • fine-tip permanent ink pen • scissors • Paintbox inkpad assortment • Peerless Watercolor paper cards • colored permanent ink pens • mini stapler • cosmetic sponges • water brushes • alphabet stamps • mini pump-top water bottle • pre-painted background paper • tape • 3" × 5" (8cm × 13cm) index cards (loose or spiral-bound) • your Personal Palette • your Prompt Tag Journal

Start TODAY
This is the beginning of something GREAT.
Travel. Art. US. what

Expansion Kit

The expansion set would include these additional items:

gel medium • acrylic paint in primary colors plus black and white • ruler • flat brush • shipping tags • paper punches • favorite rubber stamps • decorative paper

With either the essentials or expanded kit, you can create directly in your journal or make pages to glue into your journal later. We like to bring pre-painted background pages with us for journaling on the go with just the essentials on hand. Later, the pages go in a journal box or a book. These supplies easily fit in a plastic snap-and-seal container that you can take anywhere and shove under your bed when you are at home!

Stranded / Laugh

I made this page while we were on a trip, using pre-painted background paper I brought with me. The handwritten words, combined with stamping and cutout text, add playfulness and personality. The vertical placement of text adds an unexpected twist. The swirling, muted shapes in the background accent the text without being overbearing.—Linda

We are Stranded.
Karen forgot her
passport, her keys + her
B R A I N.
The GOOD news is
that we see
donuts + we
have money.

LAUGH!

Resources

Supplies

Clearsnap, Inc.
P.O. Box 98
Anacortes, WA 98221
www.clearsnap.com
*ColorBox Petal Point and
Paintbox Inkpads*

Creative Chaos Rubber Stamps
P.O. Box 3695
Fontana, CA 92334
www.vickieenkoff.com
Rubber stamps

My Daughter's Wish
1475 North Broadway, Suite 185
Walnut Creek, CA 94596
www.mydaughterswish.com
*Premier dealer of
Audmatic rubber stamps*

Peerless Watercolor
11 Diamond Place
Rochester, NY 14609
www.peerlesscolor.com
*Watercolor paints in a
booklet form*

Queen-of-Tarts Rubber Stamps
P.O. Box 3803
Hillsboro, OR 97123
www.queen-of-tarts.com
Rubber stamps

Stewart Superior
www.stewartsuperior.com
Memories Inkpads

Treetop Publishing
P.O. Box 085567
Racine, WI 53408
www.barebooks.com
*Journals and sketchbooks—
from small to really BIG*

The Watermark Bindery
P.O. Box 273
Port Townsend, WA 98368
www.thewatermarkbindery.com
Journals and sketchbooks

Contributing Artists

Jennifer Black, page 115
jblackdesigns@gmail.com
www.itsmysite.com/jblack

Judy Claxton, page 109

Emily Dinino, page 111

Sujata Easton, page 107

Lee Goldberg, page 106
www.leegoldberg.com

Marlene Hazlewood, page 109

Ronda Kivett, page 114
ronda@kivett-studio.com
www.kivett-studio.com

Emmy Tofa, page 113
tofa097@bellsouth.net
www.itsmysite.com/emmytofa

Erika Tysse, page 115
erikatysse@lyse.net
www.erikatysse.com

Dustin Woods, page 107

Good Eats

Barbara's Cake
www.visualchronicles.com/
thecake.htm
*The Ultimate Chocolate
Obsession Cake*

Fran's Chocolates, Ltd.
1300 East Pike Street
Seattle, WA 98122
www.franschocolates.com
Coconut Gold Bar

Nutella (Ferrero USA, Inc.)
600 Cottontail Lane
Somerset, NJ 08873
www.nutellausa.com
Nutella

See's Candy Shops, Inc.
20600 South Alameda Street
Carson, CA 90810
www.sees.com
*Milk chocolate Bordeaux,
chocolate butter cream,
peanut brittle*

Starbucks
P.O. Box 3717
Seattle, WA 98124-3717
www.starbucks.com
Chantico, Mocha Frappuccino

Thai 'N I Restaurant
17544 Ventura Boulevard
Encino, CA 91316
*Barbequed ribs, pad Thai,
fried rice*

Trader Joe's
www.traderjoes.com
Bread, hummus, spinach dip

Index

South East Essex College
of Arts & Technology
Luker Road, Southend-on-Sea Essex SS1 1ND
Tel:(01702) 220400 Fax:(01702) 432320 Minicom: (01702) 22064.

Indulge your creative side with these inspiring North Light Books!

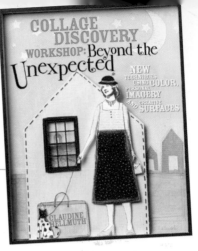

Collage Discovery Workshop: Beyond the Unexpected

CLAUDINE HELLMUTH

In a follow-up to her first workshop book, Claudine Hellmuth taps into a whole new level of creativity in *Beyond the Unexpected*. Inside you'll find original artwork and inventive ideas that show you how to personalize your own collage pieces using new techniques and interesting surfaces. In addition, the extensive gallery compiled by Claudine and other top collage artists will spark your imagination. Whether you're a beginner or a collage veteran, you'll enjoy this lovely book both as inspiration and as a practical guide.

ISBN 1-58180-535-7 paperback 128 pages #33267

Art Stamping Workshop

GLORIA PAGE

Create a signature look with stamped images you carve yourself! *Art Stamping Workshop* introduces you to the world of carving and printing soft blocks to create great gifts, home décor items and personal apparel—all with a look uniquely yours. Detailed instructions on carving tools and techniques get you started. Then you'll create 20 projects on paper, fabric and alternative surfaces, such as wood and polymer clay. Discover the fulfillment that comes from printing your own images and start carving your stamps today!

ISBN 1-58180-696-5 paperback 128 pages #33355

Altered Books Workshop

BEV BRAZELTON

A book isn't just a book anymore—it can have windows, doors, drawers and more. *Altered Books Workshop* gives you comprehensive instruction and inspiration for creating multi-dimensional art that is a reflection of your moods, thoughts and life. You'll learn how to turn old books into dazzling works of art by combining mixed media and papercrafting techniques with elements of collaging, journaling, rubber stamping and scrapbooking. You'll love learning the wide range of creative techniques for crafting unique, personalized altered books offered through the over 50 projects and ideas inside *Altered Books Workshop*.

ISBN 1-58180-535-7 paperback 128 pages #32889

These and other fine North Light titles are available from your local art and craft retailer, bookstore or online supplier.

Books Unbound

MICHAEL JACOBS

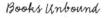

The clever ideas and techniques in *Books Unbound* take traditional bookbinding methods outside of the box and into the realm of limitless possibilities. You'll delight in the energetic innovation and never-before-seen effects that explore the creative potential of paper and pages. Complete step-by-step instruction shows you how to create pop-up designs, multiple layers and sculptural, special folds in a nontraditional approach to making books.

ISBN 1-58180-718-X paperback 128 pages #33391